Stitch by Stitch

Volume 1

TORSTAR BOOKS

NEW YORK · TORONTO

Stitch by Stitch

TORSTAR BOOKS INC.
300 E. 42ND STREET,
NEW YORK, NY 10017

Knitting and crochet abbreviations

approx = approximately	in = inch(es)	sl st = slip stitch
beg = begin(ning)	inc = increas(e)(ing)	sp = space(s)
ch = chain(s)	K = knit	st(s) = stitch(es)
cm = centimeter(s)	oz = ounce(s)	tbl = through back of
cont = continue(ing)	P = purl	loop(s)
dc = double crochet	patt = pattern	tog = together
dec = decreas(e)(ing)	psso = pass slipped	tr = triple crochet
dtr = double triple	stitch over	WS = wrong side
foll = follow(ing)	rem = remain(ing)	wyib = with yarn in
g = gram(s)	rep = repeat	back
grp = group(s)	RS = right side	wyif = with yarn in front
hdc = half double	sc = single crochet	yd = yard(s)
crochet	sl = slip	yo = yarn over

A guide to the pattern sizes

		10	12	14	16	18	20
Bust	in	32½	34	36	38	40	42
	cm	83	87	92	97	102	107
Waist	in	25	26½	28	30	32	34
	cm	64	67	71	76	81	87
Hips	in	34½	36	38	40	42	44
	cm	88	92	97	102	107	112

Torstar Books also offers a range of acrylic book stands, designed to keep instructional books such as *Stitch by Stitch* open, flat and upright while leaving the hands free for practical work.

For information write to Torstar Books Inc., 300 E.42nd Street, New York, NY 10017.

Library of Congress Cataloging in Publication Data
Main entry under title:

Stitch by stitch.

Includes index.
1. Needlework. I. Torstar Books (Firm)
TT705.S74 1984   746.4   84-111
ISBN 0-920269-00-1 (set)

98765

ISBN 0-920269-01-X (Volume 1)

Contents

Introduction

With your first volume of *STITCH BY STITCH: A Home Needlecraft Library* you begin a creative adventure that will last a lifetime. From now on you will be able to turn out beautiful fashions, accessories, home decorations and gifts in the colors and materials you prefer, and at prices that make sense.

Whatever your current level of skill in the various needlecrafts — rank beginner or whiz kid — you will find these attractive books uniquely tailored to your needs.

Perhaps you've never done any crocheting, knitting or sewing at all. Or did you take it up once, and then drop it? No matter. Everything you should know to become an accomplished needlecrafter is presented in clear, step-by-step courses, illustrated with full-color photos or drawings.

If you are already an old hand at one or more of the skills taught, you will still find the STITCH BY STITCH courses a valuable refresher particularly for clarifying certain techniques on which you may be a bit rusty. Especially for you, though, are our Extra Special projects in all the disciplines taught. Challenging, original and truly lovely items to knit, sew or crochet have been selected that will make a lasting impression on family and friends. In the Homemaker sections, too, you can put your talents to work on a host of clever and practical decorations and soft furnishings.

First, however, let's take a closer look at the Courses.

CROCHET

Crochet is an endlessly versatile skill, as more and more people are discovering. The word comes from the French *croc* which means hook—the tool with which crocheting is done. Crochet, like knitting, is a looped fabric produced from a single, continuous length of yarn. The difference is that knitting uses at least two needles, onto which a number of stitches are cast, whereas crochet uses just the one hook, working a single stitch at a time.

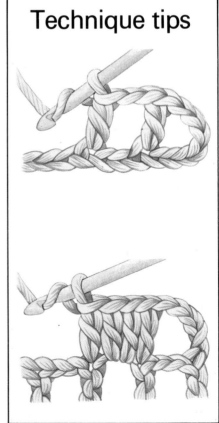

Technique tips

The Step-by-Step Crochet Course is designed to introduce you to the whole range of delightful textures and effects in easy stages. You'll see how basic stitches develop into simple fabrics; how to make circles, squares and wheels; how to use color in stripes, chevrons and checks.

There are techniques for making airy-light lace and gorgeous, chunky patchwork; for working the traditional Irish motifs and the unusual Tunisian crochet which incorporates techniques similar to knitting. We illustrate how to make beautiful edgings, braids and fringes, how to crochet on net and how to create stunning crochet beadwork.

These and many more techniques are covered in step-by-step photographs — and, of course, the graded pattern at each stage means you always have something at just the right level to try out your new stitches and skills. There are patterns for all ages, from baby wear to fashion wear.

EXTRA SPECIAL CROCHET

Really good, modern crochet patterns are always so hard to find. These carefully selected ones let you put into practice the skills you have learned so that you get professional-looking results. We show you how to get the best out of the many exciting and different modern yarns available, from cool cottons to glittery novelty yarns; the special Technique tips that accompany each pattern will enhance your knowledge of the craft. So, welcome to a world where *filet, hairpin* and *broomstick* have bright new meanings. You're on your way to making the most of new and traditional stitches.

KNITTING

If you've always wanted to be able to knit, the Step-by-Step Knitting Course will show you how. Even if you've never picked up a needle before, you'll soon know how to pick up stitches — and you'll be surprised how quickly you can take on real patterns.

Each stage of the knitting course has one or more patterns that you can make with just the stitches and techniques covered up to that point in the course. At first, they are plain and simple projects requiring no shaping. Then, as you progress from the basic techniques of casting on, knitting and purling, stockinette stitch, increasing and decreasing, gauge, picking up dropped stitches, making, selvage

edges and casting off to rather more advanced work — the wonderful textures of ribbing, checks, ridges, basketweave, ripple, chevron, diagonal, brocade and every conceivable cable — you will find yourself able to duplicate the glamorous knitwear — pullovers, vests, cardigans, shawls — that costs a fortune in the boutiques.

You will graduate to four needles and circular needles, learn about yarn substitution, understand the intricacies of traditional Fair Isle, Aran and Shetland knitting. There are full instructions on finishing and pressing to give your garments the perfect finishing touch. Best of all, we

even show you how to design your own garments. Once you understand the basic principles, this is the most rewarding way to use your knitting skills.

EXTRA SPECIAL KNITTING

These patterns have been chosen with the experienced knitter in mind, but it does not take long to join their ranks if you follow the Step-by-Step Knitting Course faithfully. Help yourself to every color and texture of yarn, from the strong, natural oiled wools to delightful fluffy mohair, Knitted lace, following a knitting chart, working a yoke — learn all the ways to make your knitting Extra Special.

5

SEWING

The Step-by-Step Sewing Course is planned to make your dreams of superbly-fitting, stylish clothes come true — clothes that will flatter you as an individual, and clothes that will make your family prefer your handiwork to anything they could buy. In sewing, there are countless professional tricks of the trade, and we make sure you benefit from them all.

Each stage of the course covers all the skills needed to make the garment in that lesson. Through the clear, step-by-step photographs you are shown how to use a sewing machine properly; how to understand and cope with paper patterns; and how to alter a pattern to fit properly. The dressmaking techniques required to insert sleeves, to fit collars and cuffs, to make gathers, pleats, facings and fastenings are made as easy as possible to follow. And with STITCH BY STITCH there's never any rush. You do things at the pace you choose. What might seem daunting tasks for the uninitiated are, in fact, steadily accomplished, simply by taking one clear step at a time.

Those finer details, like how to get the buttonhole right and how to put in a zipper so that it is completely concealed, are thoroughly explained with the help of just the right pictures. As your skills develop, we show you how to alter basic pattern pieces to get a truly custom-designed look. Your volumes of STITCH BY STITCH come with free patterns to accompany the making-up directions found in certain lessons. The dressmaker's sizes 10 to 20 correspond to sizes 8 to 18 in ready-made clothes.

EXTRA SPECIAL SEWING

In Extra Special Sewing the emphasis is on designs that you cut and sew, but which need no paper patterns. We include a wide variety of clothes to suit all the family. See how to create different looks by changing fabric, trimmings and accessories. Machine appliqué, easy embroidery or patchwork enliven these and other simple garments already in your wardrobe.

NEEDLEWORK

The most ornamental of all needlecrafts must be embroidery. The Step-by-Step Needlework Course (a shorter, bonus course to supplement your main skills at crochet, knitting and sewing) introduces you to the traditional pleasures of the 'gentle' needle arts that are quickly regaining their former popularity. Needlepoint is a firm favorite which this course covers in detail, and you will find instruction right across the wide, colorful range of patchwork, cross-stitch, appliqué, quilting, cutwork, beading and pulled thread techniques. Starting with the basics, each lesson increases your range of stitches. Both machine and free-style handwork are included. Projects in this course include home accessories as well as clothes. Try your hand at a wallhanging or an embroidered blouse. Needlework is as relaxing as it is rewarding. You'll soon discover how satisfying it is to create your own heirlooms.

HOMEMAKER

Your crochet, knitting, sewing and needlework skills can be applied to far more than lovely clothes. Use them to give individual flair to your home, filling it with the special designer touches for which other people have to pay handsomely.

You will find detailed patterns for making a great variety of home accessories. Every design we have included is set out in clear, step-by-step instructions and diagrams — mini-courses, if you like — that teach you how to make such basic items as curtains, bed linen, slipcovers and lampshades. You will discover a wealth of projects great and small — elegant cushions and pillows, tablecloths, napkins, placemats, window blinds, rugs — in fact everything for bed, bath, table and window.

In addition there are many original ideas for gifts, as well as a superb selection of soft toys, dolls and puppets. The Homemaker section truly has something for everyone, with the opportunity to bring all your needlecraft skills together.

Now you can fill your home with exactly the colors and textures that express your personality best, and save money too!

Terry Evans

SHOESTRING

Scattered throughout your volumes of STITCH BY STITCH you'll find these fun little "extras" — items that can be made quickly for next to nothing, often using scraps and remnants from your more important projects. The Shoestring ideas are long on imagination, short on expense — what could be more appealing? From scented sachets to amusing mobiles, you can make marvelous things both to keep and to give.

A PROJECT FINDER INDEX

To accompany your complete 20-volume library of STITCH BY STITCH you will receive a double index. The first is a comprehensive, alphabetical listing of all the projects and techniques covered. The second is a thematic index under the headings of Crochet, Knitting, Sewing, Needlework and Homemaker, listing the projects by category, such as evening wear, baby clothes, sportswear, accessories and so on. The dual index makes it twice as easy to find just what you're looking for, and to make the most of STITCH BY STITCH.

Crochet

Step-by-step course—1

* The basis of crochet
* Making a single crochet fabric
* Keeping the edge neat and straight
* Joining a new ball of yarn
* Checking stitch gauge
* Throw pillows to make

Crochet is one of the most versatile and exciting skills to learn. If you need inspiration, look at the samples on this page . . . just a few of the beautiful modern and traditional patterns you can create. Once you've mastered the basic stitches, it's an easy skill to develop and very quick to work.

Hooks

Crochet hooks are made in a range of sizes from the slender No. 14 steel hook, used for fine lace crochet, through a series of aluminum hooks from size B to size K for ordinary yarns, to the giant wooden size 15 and plastic size Q for very bulky yarns. The size is determined by the measurement around the body of the shaft.

Yarns

Most yarns can be used for crochet, from very fine cotton thread used in lace crochet to the really thick, bulky yarns. It is best to buy all the yarn you will need for a particular design at the same time, to ensure that all of it comes from the same dye lot; colors from different dye lots vary considerably and this will show up badly on the finished fabric. Yarn is sold in either ounces (grams) or yards.

Alan Duns

The basis of crochet

1 To make a slip knot, first wind the yarn around your fingers like this.

5 Wind the yarn over the left hand fingers. This is the recommended way, but as you practice you will find your own most comfortable position.

Making a single crochet fabric

Single crochet is the smallest stitch used in crochet. It gives a firm, closely woven fabric, with a pretty, seeded look, which is equally attractive worked in a fine or bulky yarn.

Before beginning to work any crochet stitches, extra chains are made in order to bring the hook up to the same height as the stitch being worked and to give the fabric a straight edge. They are always counted as the first stitch of every row and are called the *turning chain*.

4 Wind the yarn clockwise around the hook as before.

2 Slide a piece of yarn through the first loop.

3 Pull through the yarn to form a slip knot and a loop. Put the loop on the crochet hook and pull it tight.

4 Hold the hook in your right hand as you would a pencil, keeping the thumb and first finger as close to the hook as possible. Rest the shank against the second finger.

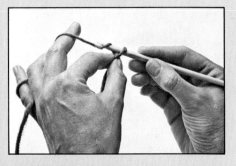

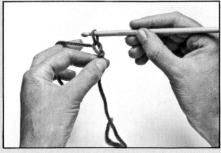

6 Hold the slip knot firmly in the left hand and wind the yarn in a clockwise direction over the shaft and around the hook.

7 Draw the yarn through the loop on the hook. This makes one chain stitch.

8 Repeat steps 6 and 7 to make as many chains as you need. Always hold the chain as close to the hook as possible with the thumb and first finger of the left hand.

1 Make a chain of any length. Insert the hook from front to back into the third chain from hook. The two skipped chains are the turning chain.

2 Wind the yarn clockwise around the hook.

3 Draw the loop through the chain. There are now two loops on the hook.

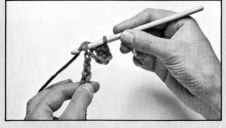

5 Draw the yarn through the two loops on the hook. One single crochet made.

6 Insert the hook from front to back into the next chain.

7 Repeat steps 2-5 to make a single crochet. *continued*

David Levin   Paul Williams

8 Continue to work one single crochet into each chain until you reach the end of the row.

9 To turn your work keep the hook in the right hand and turn the crochet over from right to left.

10 Work one turning chain, which counts as the first stitch. Skip the first stitch and work into the second stitch in order to keep the edge of your work straight.

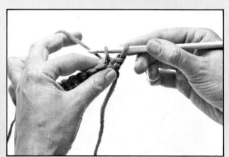

11 Insert hook from front to back into the second stitch *under* the two horizontal loops at the top.

12 Wind the yarn around the hook as in step 2.

13 Draw through the loop as in step 3.

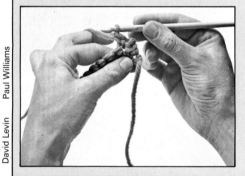

14 Wind yarn over the hook again and pull through to complete the first single crochet of the new row. Repeat to end.

15 Work the last single crochet into the turning chain of the previous row. Do this on every row to keep the edge straight.

16 After working required rows, fasten off by cutting the yarn, drawing end through last loop at end of row, pulling tight, and darning in loose end with yarn needle.

Keeping the edge neat and straight

When you begin working a crochet fabric you may find it difficult to keep the edges straight. Don't worry—this is a common mistake. It happens because you are not working into the correct stitches at each end of the row. Remember to make a turning chain at the beginning of the row, work into the second stitch, skipping the first stitch as in step 10. Work the last stitch into the turning chain at the end of the row as in step 15.

1 The fabric will slant inward if you do not work into the turning chain at the end of the row.

2 The fabric will get wider if you do not skip the first stitch and work into the second stitch.

Joining a new ball of yarn

A new ball of yarn should always be joined to the fabric at the side of the work, and never in the middle of a row. If you reach the middle of the row and have insufficient yarn to complete it, take the hook out of the working loop and rip out the stitches back to the side edge. Pick up the working loop to join the new yarn. Correct mistakes by ripping out stitches in the same way.

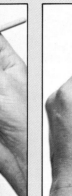

1 Work to end of the row in the usual way until the two loops of the last stitch are on the hook.

2 Hold the fabric and yarn in left hand and loop the new yarn around the hook.

3 Draw new yarn through the two loops on hook. This completes the stitch and introduces the new yarn.

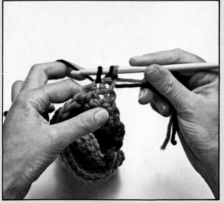

4 Turn work. Hold the old and new yarn together and work the turning chain with both yarns together to hold the new yarn in place. Pull the loose ends to tighten the stitch.

5 Work the next stitch using only the new yarn.

6 Continue working with new yarn. When you have finished the piece, come back to the two loose ends and darn in, using a blunt-ended yarn needle.

Stitch gauge

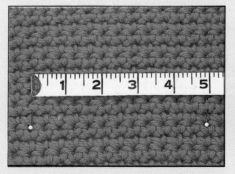

To make sure that your crochet work is the correct size when completed, you should always work a gauge sample with the hook and yarn suggested. If necessary you can change your gauge by changing the hook size. Keep changing the hook size until your gauge is correct.
Example: Your directions call for a gauge of 12 stitches to 4in (10cm) using a size H hook and bulky yarn. Make a sample with at least 24 stitches, 4in (10cm) deep. Mark off 12 stitches with pins. Pin the sample flat and then measure your 12 stitches.

If the 12 stitches measure more than 4in (10cm) your work is too loose; change to a smaller hook.

If the 12 stitches measure less than 4in (10cm) your work is too tight; you must change to a larger hook.

Throw pillows

Practice your stitches on one of these simple pillows, or maybe two or three . . . a colorful collection for your house or garden.

Size:
We give specific directions to fit a pillow form 16in (41cm) square (available in most needlework departments).

Materials:
For 1 cover in knitting worsted, approx 7oz (180g) yarn
Size F (4.00mm) crochet hook
For 1 cover in bulky knitting yarn, approx 12oz (340g) yarn
Size H (5.50mm) crochet hook
1 pillow form 16in (41cm) square for each pillow

1 Make 69 chains for knitting worsted or 55 for bulky knitting yarn.

2 Continue working in rows of single crochet, with 68 single crochets in each row for knitting worsted, or 54 in each row for bulky knitting yarn.

3 Work until fabric measures 15in (38cm) from beginning. Fasten off.

4 Darn in all loose ends of yarn using a blunt-ended yarn needle. Make another piece in the same way.

5 Using either the same knitting worsted, or a thinner yarn in a matching color for bulky knitting yarn, overcast around three sides of pillow.

6 Insert pillow form into cover. Overcast remaining seam.

To make a cover for an existing pillow, measure the width and depth of your pillow and make the cover 1in (2.5cm) less all around. **Example:** for a pillow measuring 14in (35.5cm) square you will need a 13in (33cm) square cover.

To work out the number of stitches for any size cover: make a sample piece approximately 4in (10cm) square in the stitch and yarn you are using. Count the stitches in 2in (5cm).

Example: If you have 5 stitches to 2in (5cm) you will need to make 33 chains plus two extra for the turning chain for a 13in (33cm) cover.

Peter Pugh-Cook

Crochet / COURSE 2

Making a half double crochet fabric

1 Make a chain of any length. Wind yarn clockwise around the hook.

2 Insert the hook from front to back into the third chain from the hook. First two are turning chains.

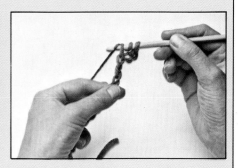

3 Wind the yarn around the hook.

4 Draw the yarn through the chain. There are now three loops on the hook.

5 Wind the yarn around the hook and draw it through all three loops on the hook. One half double has been made.

6 Repeat these steps into each chain to the end.

7 Turn work. Make *two* chains.

8 Skip the first stitch. Work the first half double as before into the second stitch. Work one half double into each stitch to the end of the row.

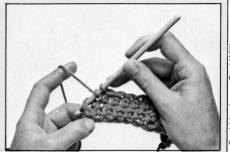

9 Work the last half double into the turning chain of the previous row. Repeat these last three steps for the number of rows you need.

David Levin   Paul Williams

13

The cozy baby bag

Warm as toast for chilly days — a snug sleeping bag worked in half doubles

John Hawkins

turning chain of previous row. Turn. Continue working in rows of half-doubles in this way until back measures 22in (56cm). Draw yarn through and fasten.

Left front

Using size H (5.50mm) hook, chain 18. Work 1 half-double into 3rd chain from hook, 1 half-double into each chain to end. Turn. 17 half-doubles.
Continue working in rows of half-doubles as given for back.
Work until left front measures same as back. Draw yarn through and fasten off.

Right front

Using size H (5.50mm) hook, chain 24. Work 1 half-double into 3rd chain from hook, 1 half-double into each chain to end. Turn. 23 half-doubles.
Continue working in rows of half-doubles until right front measures same as back. Draw yarn through and fasten off.

Sleeves

Using size H (5.50mm) hook, chain 24. Work 1 half-double into each chain to end of row. 23 half-doubles.
Continue working in half-doubles until sleeve measures 5¼in (13.5cm). Draw yarn through and fasten off.

Base

Using size H (5.50mm) hook make 9 chain. Work 1 half-double into 3rd chain from hook. 1 half-double into each chain to end. Turn 8 half-doubles.
Continue working in rows of half-doubles until piece measures 13½in (34cm). Draw yarn through and fasten.

To finish

☐ With right sides together pin front pieces to the back with right front overlapping left front by 2in (5cm).
☐ Using a flat seam (see page 29) throughout join right and left shoulder seams for 3½in (9cm) at each side. Mark a point 3½in (9cm) from shoulder on side seams for armholes. With right sides together, sew sleeve tops in position along armhole openings.
☐ Join side and sleeve seams.
☐ Join right front to left front on the outside, for 3½in (9cm) from bottom edge where they overlap. Sew the left front to the right front on the inside.
☐ Pin the base to the bottom of the bag matching side seams of bag with centers of base ends.
☐ Sew in place using a flat seam.
☐ Sew two snap fasteners at the inner and outer edges of the left front at the neck edge to hold in place. Repeat 3 more times at even intervals down the front.
☐ Thread ribbon through the last row of half-doubles on the sleeves and draw up. Tie a bow at neck edge on right front at same place as snaps if desired.

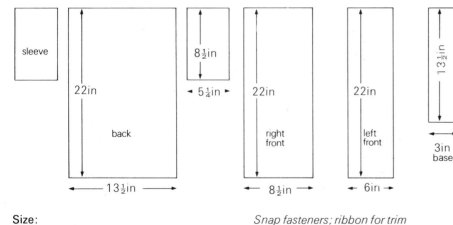

Size:

Up to 6 months. Length to shoulder, 22in (56cm). Sleeve seam, 5¼in (13.5cm).

Gauge

11 stitches and 9 rows to 4in (10cm) in half doubles on size H (5.50mm) hook.

Materials

11oz (300g) of a bulky sport yarn
1 size H (5.50mm) hook

Snap fasteners; ribbon for trim

Back

Using size H (5.50mm) hook, chain 38. Work 1 half-double into 3rd chain from hook, then 1 half-double into each chain to end. Turn, 37 half-doubles worked.
Next row Chain 2 to count as first half-double, skip first stitch, work a half-double into next and every stitch to end of row. Work last half-double into

Crochet / COURSE 3

*Making a double-crochet fabric
*Joining with double crochet
*Patterns for adult's and child's scarf

Making a double-crochet fabric

A double is the first of the long stitches used in crochet. It makes a more open fabric than single crochet and produces a lattice effect when used with fine yarns. In filet crochet blocks of doubles are worked to form motifs over an open lattice background, and doubles can be used with single crochet and half-doubles to make shaped motifs such as shells.

Making a double-crochet

Since the double is a much longer stitch than a single crochet, it is necessary to work three turning chains at the beginning of every row. Work the last stitch of every row into the top of the three turning chain of the previous row to keep the edge straight, and to prevent the yarn from pulling the work out of shape at the side edge.

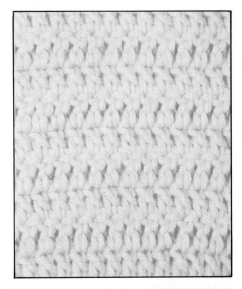

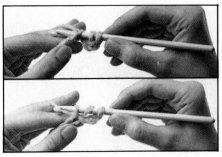

1 Make any number of chains, making two more chains than the number of stitches you will need, i.e. for 30 stitches make 32 chains. Wind the yarn around the hook. Insert the hook from front to back into fourth chain from hook.
2 Wind the yarn around the hook and draw through a loop. Three loops on hook.

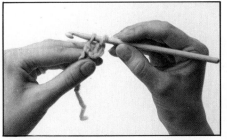

3 Wind the yarn around the hook and draw it through the first two loops on the hook. Two loops remain on hook.

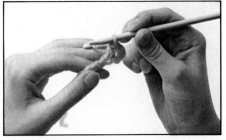

4 Wind the yarn around the hook and draw it through the last two loops on the hook. One double has been made.

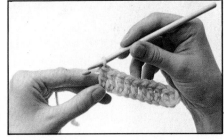

5 Work one double in the same way into each chain to the end of the row.

6 Turn work. Work three turning chains. Skip the first stitch. Work the first double into the second stitch.

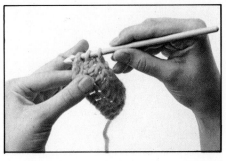

7 Work into each double to end, working the last double into the top of the turning chain of the previous row.

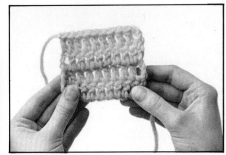

8 Continue to work in this way for the number of rows you need. Fasten off.

Joining with single crochet

A decorative seam can be made by joining two pieces of fabric with single crochet. Make a feature of the seam by using yarn in a contrasting color. When worked on the wrong side of the fabric, the seam gives a laced appearance on the right side.

1 Pin two pieces of fabric to be joined together just below the edge of the seam.

2 Insert hook through both thicknesses of fabric.

3 Loop the yarn around the hook and draw it through.

4 Work one chain with both ends of yarn and pull firmly to hold it in place.

5 Work one chain, one single crochet into next row, end just below the edge.

6 Continue to work one single crochet into each row end to the end of the seam. Draw yarn through and fasten off.

7 When working with a double fabric, work three stitches into every two row ends.

8 One chain can be worked between each stitch to spread the stitches along the seam.

Scarves for all the family

Scarves that look good on all ages, worked in stitches you have learned so far. Turn up the bottom to make pockets and join with a decorative single-crochet seam, or fold the scarf in half and join the edges at the center to make a cozy hood.

Scarf with pockets

Child's scarf measures about $6\frac{3}{4}$ x 48in (17 x 122cm) with pockets turned back.
Adult's scarf measures 8 x 67in (20 x 170cm) with pockets turned back.

Gauge
17 sts to 4in (10cm) in doubles worked on a Size F (4.00mm) hook.

Note Follow the figures in brackets [ ] for the adult's scarf.

Materials
8[9]oz (200[250]g) sport yarn
Size F (4.00mm) hook
Small quantity of contrasting color
yarn (optional)

To make scarf
Using a Size F (4.00mm) hook make 30 [36] chains.
☐ Work 1 double into 4th chain from hook, 1 double into each chain to end of row. 28 [34] doubles.
☐ Continue working in rows of doubles working 3 turning chains at the beginning of every row until work measures 61 [86] (154.5 [219]cm) or the length you require. Fasten off. Darn in all ends.

To make pockets
Turn 5¾ [9] in (14.5 [23]cm) up at each end to form pockets and pin into place. Join the pockets with single crochet.
☐ Work from right to left with the pocket facing you and folded edge to the right. Using a Size F (4.00mm) hook and contrasting color yarn, insert hook from front to back through both thicknesses of scarf. Loop the yarn over the hook and draw a loop through. Work 1 chain using both ends of yarn to hold the stitch in place. Now working with 1 end of yarn only, work * 1 chain, 1 single crochet into the next row end. Repeat from * to the end of the pocket, working the last single crochet into the corner of the pocket.
☐ Work the other side of the pocket beginning from the top edge of the pocket so that the front of the single crochet shows on the same side of the pocket.
☐ Work the other side of the pocket in the same way. Darn in all ends.
☐ Press scarf according to the directions on the yarn wrapper.

George Wright

Scarf with hood

Size
Child's scarf measures 6¾ x 56in (17 x 142.5cm).
Adult's scarf measures 9 x 63¾in (23 x 162cm).

Gauge
17 sts to 4in (10cm) in single crochet worked on a Size F (4.00mm) hook.

Materials
7[10]oz (175[275]g) of a sport
yarn
Size F (4.00mm) hook

Note Follow the figures in brackets [ ] for the adult's scarf.

To make scarf
Using a Size F (4mm) hook make 30 [41] chains.
☐ Work 1 single crochet into 3rd chain from hook, 1 single crochet into each chain to end. 29 [40] single crochet.
☐ *Work stripes of 1¼in (3cm) single crochet, 2in (5cm) half-double, 2¾in (7cm) double, 2in (5cm) half-double. Repeat from * until work measures 56 [63¾]in (142.5 [162]cm) or length you require, ending with 1¼in (3cm) single crochet. Fasten off. Darn in all ends.
☐ Fold the scarf in half and pin seam together at center for 7 [8½]in (18 [22] cm) to form hood.

To join with single crochet
☐ Insert the hook from front to back at center fold through both thicknesses of the scarf just below the edge of the seam. Loop the yarn over the hook and draw the yarn through. Wind 2 thicknesses of yarn around hook and draw through the loop to hold the yarn in place. Continue working through both thicknesses working 2 single crochet into each row end, for 7 [8½]in (18 [22]cm). Draw yarn through and fasten off. Darn in all ends.
☐ Press the scarf according to the instructions on the yarn wrapper.

Crochet / COURSE 4

*Achieving correct gauge
*Checking your gauge
*Using a substitute yarn

Achieving correct gauge

Now that you have mastered the basic stitches in crochet it is vital to understand the importance of obtaining the "correct gauge" when working a pattern, as this can mean the difference between success and failure.

By "correct gauge" we mean working the same number of stitches and rows in the same measurement as the designer of the pattern used. This measurement is usually 4in (10cm). Although you may not get the same number of stitches to begin with, this does not mean that your work is "wrong," but simply that you make stitches slightly looser or slightly tighter than the designer. This is due to the tension which you exert on your yarn when making loops. The difference in the gauge can easily be remedied by changing to a different size hook.

Before beginning to work on a pattern the designer will crochet a square using the hook, yarn and stitch intended for the project. The number of stitches in this square will determine the size and shape of the finished project as all the measurements for it will be calculated from this figure. You must achieve the same gauge as that used in the directions or the project will not turn out the same size as the original. Remember that a difference of even one stitch over 4in (10cm) can alter the size of the finished fabric.

It is sometimes difficult to achieve the correct gauge in both the stitches and rows, but it is more important to get the number of stitches right, since this determines the project's width. Controlling the length of the project is much easier, since it can be altered simply by working more or fewer rows, depending on the requirements.

Checking your gauge

The gauge quoted for this pattern is 15 stitches and 13 rows to 4in (10cm) over half doubles worked in knitting worsted using a size F (4.00mm) hook.

1 Make a gauge swatch using the hook, yarn and stitch given in the pattern.

2 The gauge is measured over 4in (10cm), so make the sample at least 4in (10cm) square so you can check it correctly.

3 Pin the sample on a flat surface without stretching the stitches.

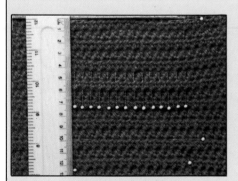

4 This sample has only 14 stitches to 4in (10cm) instead of the 15 quoted, so change to a smaller hook.

5 This sample has 20 stitches to 4in (10cm), which is too many, so change to a larger hook.

6 Keep on changing to a smaller or larger hook until you achieve the correct gauge.

Paul Williams

Using a substitute yarn

If you are unable to buy the kind of yarn suggested in your pattern it may be possible to use a substitute, but it must be as near a match as possible.

To check your gauge, work a 4in (10cm) swatch using the stitch and hook suggested, and measure to see if you need a larger or smaller hook size. If, by changing the hook size, you are able to obtain exactly the same gauge as quoted you may use the substitute yarn, although the project will, of course, look and feel different from the original.

Crochet / COURSE 5

* Making a triple crochet fabric
* Making a double triple fabric
* Easy-to-make cozy cover-up
* Pattern for a tweedy-look tunic

Triples and double triples, sometimes known as long triples, are two of the longest of the crochet stitches and are made by winding the yarn around the hook two or three times before beginning to work the stitch.

When worked in a thick yarn they produce an open, bulky fabric that is very quick to make. They are more frequently used in fine lace crochet with other stitches to form either an openwork fabric or an interesting pattern.

It is important to remember that the turning chain must be lengthened to bring the hook up to the height of the stitch being worked; four chains are worked for a triple and five for a double triple. The chain counts as the first stitch.

Making a triple crochet fabric

1 Make any length of chain, making three more chains than the number of stitches you need, so, for ten stitches make 13 chains. Wind the yarn clockwise twice around the hook.

2 Insert the hook from front to back into the fifth chain from the hook.

3 Wind the yarn clockwise around the hook.

4 Draw a loop through. There are now four loops on the hook.

5 Wind the yarn clockwise around the hook and draw it through the first two loops on the hook. Three loops are left on the hook.

6 Wind the yarn clockwise around the hook and draw through the next two loops on the hook. Two loops are left on hook.

7 Wind the yarn clockwise around the hook and draw it through the last two loops on the hook. One triple has been made.

8 Work one triple in the same way into each chain to end. Turn.

9 Make four turning chains.

continued

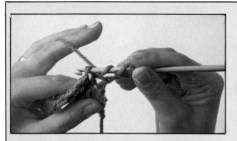

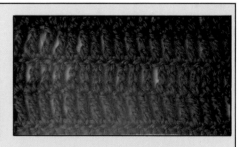

10 Skip the first stitch. Work one triple into the second stitch, working under the two horizontal loops in the normal way.

11 Work one triple into each stitch to the end of the row. Work the last triple into the top of the turning chain of the previous row.

12 Repeat the last three steps for as many rows as you need. Draw the yarn through the loop and fasten off.

Making a double triple fabric

1 Make any length of chain, making four more chains than the number of stitches you need, so, for 12 stitches make 16 chains. Wind yarn clockwise three times around the hook.

2 Insert the hook from front to back into the sixth chain from the hook. Wind yarn around the hook and draw through a loop. Five loops on the hook.

3 Wind yarn around the hook and draw it through first two loops. Four loops on the hook.

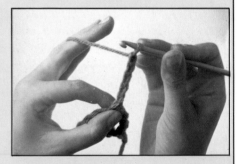

4 Repeat step 3 twice more. Two loops are left on the hook.

5 Wind yarn around the hook and draw it through last two loops on the hook. One double triple made.

6 Work one double triple in same way into each chain to end. Turn. Work five turning chains.

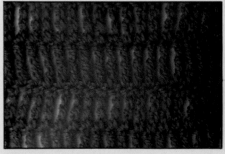

7 Skip the first stitch. Work one double triple into second stitch, working under two horizontal loops in the normal way.

8 Work one double triple into each stitch to end. Work last double triple into the top of the turning chain of the previous row.

9 Repeat the last three steps for the number of rows needed. Draw yarn through and fasten off.

Cozy cover-up

Out and about on cooler days . . . an ultra-simple crochet top
with a stylish drawstring on the hips. It's made in triple crochet
stitch – the sleeves and yoke are worked straight across from
cuff to cuff.

Belinda

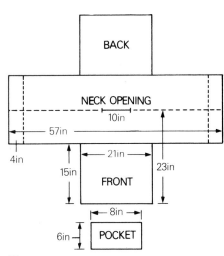

BACK

NECK OPENING

10in

57in

4in

15in   23in

FRONT

21in

8in

6in   **POCKET**

Size
To fit 34/36in (87/92cm) bust.
Length to shoulder, 23in (58cm).
Sleeve seam, 17in (43cm).
To make the top bigger add approximately 3 stitches to every 1in (2.5cm) added.

Gauge
12 sts and 4½ rows to 4ins (10cm) worked in triples on a Size G (4.50mm) hook.

Materials
23oz (650g) of a bulky yarn
Size G (4.50mm) crochet hook

Back
Using size G (4.50mm) hook make 68 chains. Work 1 triple into 5th chain from hook, then 1 triple into each chain to end. Turn. 65 triples.
☐ Continue to work in rows of triples with 4 turning chains at beginning of every row until piece measures 15in (37cm) from beginning.
☐ Draw yarn through and fasten off.

Front
Work in same way as for back.

Sleeves and yoke (worked in one piece)
Begin at cuff, work first sleeve, yoke, then second sleeve and end cuff.
☐ Using size G (4.50mm) hook make 57 chains. Work first row as given for back. 54 triples.
☐ Work in rows of triple crochet as for back until work measures 24in (61cm), ending at right-hand edge of right side of work. This will be the lower edge of front yoke.

Shape neck
Work in triple crochet on first 27 stitches only for front neck, leaving remaining 27 stitches unworked. Continue for 10in (25cm), ending at neck edge. Fasten off. Return to the last complete row worked.
☐ Rejoin yarn to remaining stitches at neck edge and work back yoke on these stitches, working the same number of rows as for front, ending at the *side edge*. Turn.
☐ Work across 27 stitches of back yoke, then across 27 stitches of front yoke. 54 stitches.

☐ Complete the yoke and sleeve on these stitches.
☐ Continue for a further 24in (61cm). Draw yarn through and fasten off.

Pocket
Using size G (4.50mm) hook make 19 chains.
☐ Work one double crochet into 3rd chain from hook, 1 double crochet into each chain to end. Turn. 18 double crochet.
☐ Work 8in (19cm) in double crochet on these stitches.
☐ Draw yarn through and fasten off.

To finish
Darn in all loose ends of yarn on wrong side of work.
☐ Mark a point with colored thread on both sleeves at front and back, 17in (43cm) from edge of cuff.
☐ Using the markers as a guide, pin the front to front yoke and the back to back yoke and sew in place using a flat seam.
☐ Join side and sleeve seams using a backstitch seam.
☐ Sew on pocket to front at top and bottom so openings are at the side. Turn back cuffs to right side.
To make the drawstring
Make a chain 50in (127cm) long.
☐ Insert hook into 2nd chain from hook and draw yarn through both loops to make 1 slip stitch. Work 1 slip stitch into each chain to end.
☐ Fasten off. Thread drawstring through triples at bottom edge and draw up.

Triple tunic

Using triple crochet stitches, make this warm tunic for cooler days and evenings. Made from two simple rectangles, the shoulders are joined with fine single crochet and the sides are laced with a cord of crochet chains.

Size
The directions are for a medium size, 34/36in (87/92cm) bust.
Length to shoulder, 27½in (70cm).
To make the tunic bigger work approximately 2 stitches more for every 1in (2.5cm) you wish to add.

Gauge
11 stitches and 4 rows to 4in (10cm) in triples on a size H (5.50mm) hook.

Materials
18oz (500g) of a bulky knitting yarn
Small quantity of knitting worsted in a contrasting color
Size H (5.50mm) hook
Size F (4.00mm) hook

Front and back sections
Using bulky yarn and size H (5.50mm) hook make 55 chains for back. Work 1 triple into 5th chain from hook, 1 triple into each chain to end. 52 triples. Continue to work in rows of triples making 4 turning chains at the beginning of every row, until the piece measures 27½in (70cm) from the beginning, measured with work flat.
Draw yarn through and fasten off. Work the front in the same way. Darn in all the loose ends on the wrong side of the work.

To work the edging
Join the bulky yarn to the right side of one piece at the shoulder edge. Using

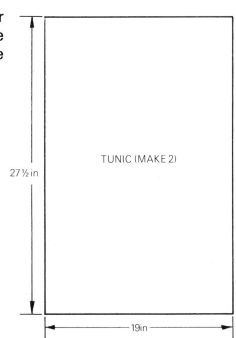

TUNIC (MAKE 2)

27½ in

19in

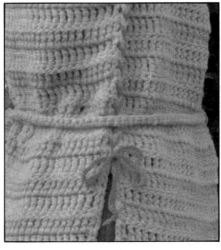

together, working into the corresponding stitches of back and front. When you have reached the shoulder edge, draw yarn through and fasten off.
Work the other shoulder in the same way, starting from the neck edge.
Darn in all the loose ends on the wrong side of the work using a yarn needle.

size H (5.50mm) hook, work 1 chain, then 1 single crochet and 1 chain down the side edge, working into the triples at the end of each row.
Work down other side edge in the same way.
Finish other piece to match.

Joining shoulders with crochet braid
By working a few rows of single crochet in a fine yarn you can obtain a braid effect on the edge of a bulky fabric, and it is possible to join two pieces together by working through the edge stitches of one piece and the braid stitches at the same time to make a contrasting seam.
With the right side of the front facing

join knitting worsted to left shoulder edge (upper right-hand corner).
Using size F (4.00mm) hook make 1 chain, then work 1 single crochet and 1 chain along the shoulder edge for about 5¼in (13.5cm).
Turn and work 1 single crochet into each single crochet, chain to the end. Then work 1 more row of single crochet. With the right side of the back facing and wrong sides together match the shoulder edges of front and back. Insert hook through back and through neck edge stitch of the edging just worked. Draw the yarn through and work a single crochet in the normal way through both thicknesses. Continue working in single crochet in this way to join the shoulder

Joining the sides with lacing
Mark a point 10¼in (26cm) from shoulder edge at each side for armholes. Using knitting worsted and size F (4.00mm) hook make 180 chains. Draw yarn through and fasten off. Make another chain in the same way. Lace the chain through the side seams to join them together for 9½in (24cm).

Optional belt
To make a belt, using size H (5.50mm) hook make a chain of bulky yarn 67in (170cm) long and work one row of single crochet, then fasten off. Make a narrow belt using size F (4.00mm) hook and one row of single crochet for the same length. Fasten off. Twist together to make belt.

Knitting

Step-by-step course—1

Classification
Many hand knitting yarns belong to groups according to their construction.

Baby and fingering yarns. Available in 3- and 4-ply weights, these yarns are soft to wear and withstand repeated washings.

Sport weight. Classic threads for general use, available in 3- and 4-ply.

Knitting worsted. A very popular hand knitting yarn; it knits up quickly into a strong fabric with many uses. It has a 4-ply construction, but each thread is about double the thickness of that used in a 4-ply sport yarn.

Bulky yarns. Much thicker than knitting worsted, this type of yarn comes in 1-, 2-, 3-, and 4-ply and makes heavy sports or outdoor garments.

Novelty yarns. Available in a wide variety of weights, these include metallic yarns, bouclés, tweeds and others. They give an unusual texture to the fabric.

Yarn
This is a term used for any type of thread used as knitting material no matter how it is made. Spinners manufacture yarn for hand knitting: it is usually sold in balls or skeins, although some very bulky yarns may come in hanks which need to be wound into balls before use.

Check the weight of the skein or ball you are buying, which varies with different types and brands. Be sure that the total weight you buy is sufficient. Since the color in different dye lots can vary quite drastically, it is essential to have enough yarn at the beginning to complete any article you want to make.

Fibers
These fall into two main categories—natural and man-made. Wool, angora, mohair, cotton and linen are all natural fibers; they are hard-wearing and pleasant to wear and handle. Some of the natural fibers are in short supply and therefore very expensive; all of them require careful hand washing.

Modern technology has given knitters new, man-made fibers such as acrylic, nylon and polyester. These are often less expensive than natural fibers and combine high bulk with light weight. They wash extremely well by hand or machine. The paper wrapper around a skein of yarn usually gives washing directions.

Wool and man-made fibers are a popular combination, giving a yarn the soft texture of wool plus the strength and washability of synthetics.

Ply
Each yarn has a "ply" classification, indicating the number of single spun threads in it. The threads are twisted together to produce yarns of recognized thickness—1-ply, 2-ply, 3-ply, 4-ply. Note that all yarns of the same ply are not necessarily the same thickness; some soft Shetland 2-plys are thicker than a fine 3- or even 4-ply yarn.

Needles

Knitting requires very few basic tools and they are all inexpensive. Needles are the main equipment necessary; these are available in a number of modern materials, such as coated aluminum and plastic, which make them light and easy to use. Old-fashioned steel needles are heavy in comparison and slow you down. To get good results take care of your needles; a bent needle distorts your fabric, an old blunt pair of needles will fray the yarn.

Sizing

Each type of yarn demands its own needle size, from very fine needles for specialty work such as lace knitting to very thick needles for heavy garments in bulky yarn. Needle sizes range from a slender No. 00 for fine thread up to No. 10½ for heavy yarns and to No. 17 for very bulky yarns.

Pair of needles

For flat knitting in rows you need a pair of needles, each with a point at one end and a knob at the other to keep the stitches from sliding off. Needles are available in two lengths — 10 and 14 inches. If there are a large number of stitches at some stage in the garment you are knitting, you'll need to use the longer length; otherwise it is more relaxing to work with shorter ones.

Needle Sizes	Yarns
No. 1-4	Baby and fingering yarns; lightweight novelty yarns
No. 1-6	Sport yarns; lightweight mohairs and bouclés; sport-weight novelty yarns
No. 4-10	Knitting worsteds; medium-weight mohairs and bouclés; knitting-worsted weight novelty yarns
No. 7-15	Craft and rug yarns; bulky yarns; heavy bouclés; Icelandic yarns; heavy novelty yarns
No. 10½-17	Super-heavy rug yarns; multi-stranded yarns; bulky novelty yarns

Sets of needles

Knitting in the round is a method of making a circular fabric without seams. It is widely used for making gloves, hats, socks, and other items that require a small number of stitches. Circular knitting needs a set of four needles with points at both ends. Three of the needles hold the stitches in a triangular shape; the fourth is used for knitting.

Circular needles

These are also for knitting in rounds, when there are too many stitches for the set of needles, or for knitting in rows where a large number of stitches are involved. The two needles are linked by a long piece of flexible plastic.

Cable needles

Cable patterns and Aran knitting require a special miniature-length straight or curved knitting needle with points at both ends. Stitches are transferred to this extra needle when you twist a cable, and held at the back or front of the knitting while you continue to work the adjacent stitches.

Stitch holders

You need these when you divide your work and leave some stitches to work later. Often they take the form of an enlarged safety pin with an open end for moving the stitches on and off and a fastening to keep the stitches from falling off the holder.

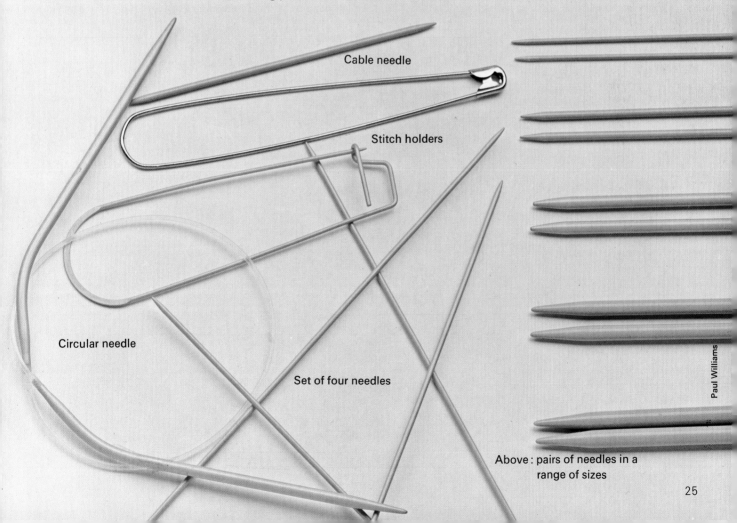

Cable needle

Stitch holders

Circular needle

Set of four needles

Paul Williams

Above: pairs of needles in a range of sizes

Knitting / COURSE 2

Casting on with two needles

All knitting starts with a foundation row of loops cast onto one needle. To make a fabric you use the second needle to build a series of interlocking loops on rows one above the other.

Generally you hold the needle with the stitches in your left hand and the needle to make the stitches in your right hand. (Left-handed people should work in reverse.) Your way of holding the yarn develops as you practice knitting: as long as you are relaxed, it is a case of personal preference. If you are in doubt, it helps to control the yarn by winding it around the fingers of your right hand so that it flows evenly, to produce a fabric with firm, even gauge.

Cast-on loops form the edge of the fabric. If the edge is tighter than the rest of your work and pulls it in, use one size larger needles for casting on only.

There are a number of different casting on methods. The two-needle method produces a firm edge and can be used for most knitted fabrics. Other ways will be covered in later courses.

Note: by FRONT we mean the side of the work nearest you;

by BACK we mean the side of the work away from you.

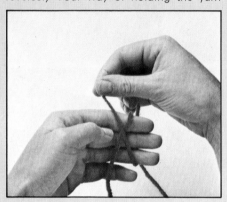

1 Start by making a slip knot with a loop about 4in from the end of the yarn.

2 Wind the yarn as indicated and pull strand through to form the loop.

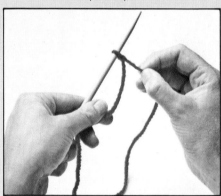

3 Place the loop on the left-hand (LH) needle; hold needle in left hand.

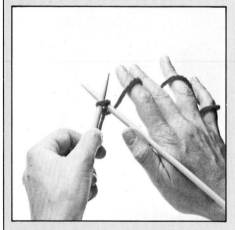

4 Hold the needle to make the stitches in your right hand.
Wind the yarn around the fingers of your right hand so that the index finger remains flexible and controls it.
Insert the right-hand (RH) needle from front to back into the loop.

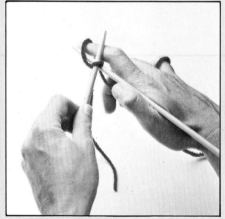

5 Wind the yarn under and over the RH needle point in a clockwise direction. Try to keep the yarn fairly loose or the cast-on edge will be too tight.

6 Pull the RH needle toward you. drawing a loop of yarn through the slip knot loop. This forms a new stitch on the RH needle.

David Levin   Paul Williams

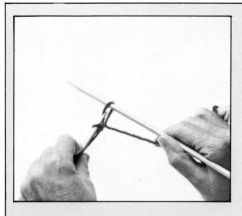

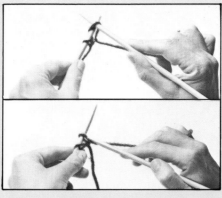

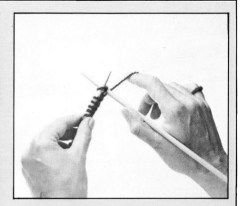

7 Twist the LH needle forward and insert the point from right to left into the front of the new stitch on the RH needle.

8 Withdraw the RH needle point; the new stitch is now transferred to the LH needle.

9 Always inserting the RH needle from front to back into the last new stitch on the LH needle, repeat steps 4-8, to cast on the number of stitches you need.

Making a garter stitch fabric

This is the easiest stitch pattern: you knit each stitch in every row to produce a fabric with textured horizontal ridges. The fabric looks the same on both sides and is therefore reversible.

A garter stitch fabric is neat and firm so that you can use it with the ridges running vertically without stretching the fabric: this creates more variety in garter stitch designs, since you can knit them from the hem up or from side edge to side edge.

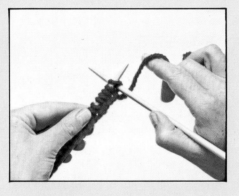

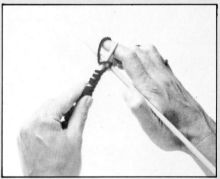

1 Hold the needle with the cast-on stitches in your left hand and the free needle in your right hand. Insert the free needle from front to back into the first stitch.

2 With the yarn at the back of the work throughout, wind it under and over the right-hand (RH) needle point.

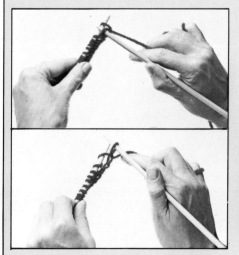

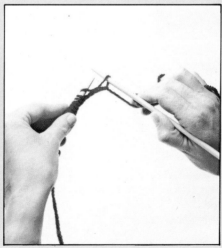

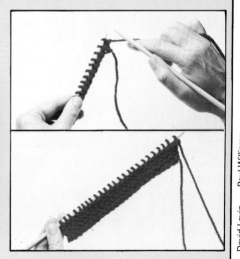

3 Pull the yarn through the stitch on the left-hand (LH) needle to make a new stitch on the RH needle.

4 Drop the stitch from the LH needle and leave the new stitch on the RH needle. Work into each of the cast-on stitches in the same way.

5 At the end of a row transfer the needles so that the one holding the stitches is in your left hand. Knit each stitch in every row to produce a garter stitch fabric.

David Levin   Paul Williams

Checking simple stitch gauge

Before beginning any pattern, you must knit a gauge sample; individuals knit with different "tightness," so checking your own gauge is the only way to make sure you obtain the exact measurements and get perfect results.

Most patterns have a gauge guide, which states the number of stitches (and often rows) to a square, usually about 4in (10cm), using the recommended yarn and needles. Concentrate on getting the correct number of stitches. The row gauge is not so important at this point, as you work to reach a given measurement, no matter how many rows it takes.

1 Look at the gauge guide at the beginning of the pattern. As an example: 12 stitches to 4in (10cm). Cast on your stitches, plus a few extra, say 17. Knit a piece at least 4in (10cm) long.

2 Count 12 stitches on your sample, and mark with pins. Lay a tape measure along the sample to check what measurement you have achieved with 12 stitches.

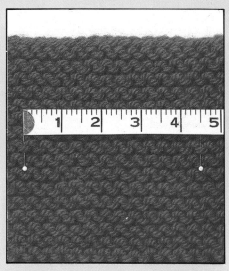

3 This work is too tight—the 12 stitches make less than 4in (10cm). Make another sample with one size larger needles: if it is still too tight, try even larger needles.

4 Here the work is too loose—the 12 stitches make more than 4in (10cm). Keep trying progressively smaller needles until you have the right gauge.

Binding off

At the end of any piece of work you must secure the stitches so that they do not unravel; do this quite loosely so that the edge does not tighten and distort the fabric.

Sometimes it is easier to make a loose edge if you use a needle one size larger to bind off the stitches on the last row.

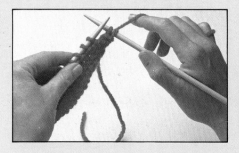

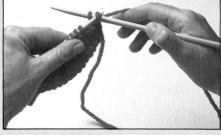

1 Knit the first two stitches in the usual way to transfer them to the RH needle.

2 Use the LH needle point to lift the first stitch over the second.

3 Push the RH needle backward with the LH index finger, at the same time drawing the stitch remaining on the RH needle through the one being lifted.

4 Withdraw the LH needle point from the stitch. One stitch remains on the RH needle, and one stitch has been bound off. Knit the next stitch on the RH needle. Insert the LH needle into the first stitch knitted and repeat the process of lifting one stitch over another.

5 Continue until one stitch remains on the RH needle. Break yarn about 4in from the work. Lengthen the loop on the needle, then drop the stitch from the needle. Draw the cut end through the loop and pull the yarn to tighten the stitch.

David Levin   Paul Williams

Joining a new ball of yarn

Measure the yarn you have left: you need about four times the width of your knitting to complete the row. If you do not have enough, do not start the row.

If your yarn does run out in the middle of a row, the best thing to do with a simple stitch is to unravel the stitches back to the beginning of the row.

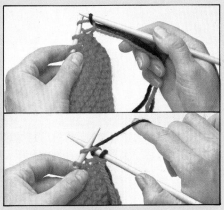

1 Insert RH needle into first stitch as usual. Leaving a piece about 4in (10cm) long, wrap the new yarn around the RH needle.

2 Pull RH needle through stitch to make first stitch in new yarn on RH needle. Insert RH needle into next stitch and wrap new yarn under and over.

3 Pull RH needle through to make second stitch: continue to knit with the new yarn. Pull ends of yarn gently to tighten edge stitches and darn in later.

Joining with a backstitch seam

This is the usual method of joining the main seams such as shoulders, side and sleeve seams on many knitted garments. Waistbands, cuffs or borders in a different stitch may require another type of seam. When working a backstitch seam, a blunt-ended yarn needle is a vital piece of equipment to avoid splitting the stitches. Pull the stitches firmly through the knitting without stretching it; at the same time do not draw the stitches up so tightly that they pucker the fabric.

The seam forms a ridge on the wrong side of the fabric that is virtually undetectable when the garment is worn. For a professional finish, press the completed seam lightly on the right side. Garter stitch garments should be pressed only *very* lightly, if at all, as pressing can destroy the texture of the fabric.

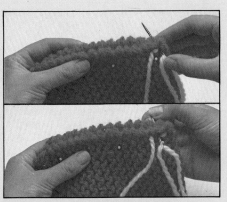

1 Place right sides together, match edges to be joined, and pin at intervals. Secure the yarn at the RH edge—about one knitted stitch in from the edge—using two small stitches, one on top of the other. Move one stitch to the left and bring the needle through from back to front.

2 Re-insert needle from front to back, at the end of the previous stitch. Bring the needle out one knitted stitch to the left. Continue like this until the seam is complete. Bind off by working two small stitches, draw the yarn a short way back along seam and cut off the extra.

Joining with a flat seam

Use this seam when you want to avoid a bulky ridge. It is equally useful whether you are working with very bulky yarn or fine yarn for baby clothes. This is also the seam to choose for joining sections of ribbing, such as waistbands or cuffs and for sewing on borders or edgings. The seam has a laced effect on the wrong side when the two pieces of knitting are laid flat.

1 Line up the two edges of knitting with right sides together, matching ridges at row ends if possible. Secure yarn at the right-hand edge through both thicknesses of fabric.

2 Overcast through corresponding ridges on each piece, being careful not to pull the yarn too tightly.

David Levin   Paul Williams

Great garter stitch!

The very basic techniques covered in this section are all you need to try your hand at a simple pattern.

Scarves are the easiest for a first attempt, but the tops, too, are simply made from straight pieces of garter stitch. Full directions are on the next page.

In all garter stitch patterns a much neater edge can be achieved by "slipping a stitch as to knit." To do this, insert the right-hand needle into the first stitch on the left-hand needle in the usual way: transfer the stitch to the right-hand needle without winding the yarn around to make a new stitch.

Scarves

Sizes
Variegated bouclé scarf is about 10 x 67in (25 x 170cm).
Mohair scarf is about 7 x 79in (18 x 200cm).
Plain scarf is about 4 x 67in (10 x 170cm).

Materials
Bouclé scarf: *12oz (340g) of a medium-weight bouclé yarn 1 pair of No. 10 (6½mm) needles*
Mohair scarf: *4oz (90g) of a medium-weight mohair yarn 1 pair of No. 15 (10mm) needles*
Plain scarf: *5oz (125g) of a bulky Aran-type knitting yarn 1 pair of No. 5 (4mm) needles*

Bouclé scarf
Cast on 35 stitches.
Work 67in (170cm) in garter stitch always slipping first stitch of every row.
Bind off.
Darn in all ends of yarn on one side of the knitting.

Mohair scarf
Cast on 18 stitches.
Work 79in (200cm) in garter stitch always slipping first stitch of every row.
The very large needles produce an open, lacy fabric.
Bind off.
Darn in all ends of yarn on one side of the knitting.

Plain scarf
Cast on 16 stitches.
Work 67in (170cm) in garter stitch always slipping first stitch of every row.
Bind off.
Darn in all ends of yarn on one side of the knitting.

Long vest

Sizes

These instructions will give a finished garment about 28¾in (73cm) long, 19in (48cm) wide across the back, 8¾in (22cm) wide across each front. These measurements allow for the weight of the yarn in garter stitch to pull the fabric slightly downward and inward. The vest fits every bust size from 32½ to 36in (83 to 92cm). To make it wider or narrower, cast on one·stitch more or less for each ⅜in (1cm) difference. Remember you may need more or less yarn according to how you adjust size.

Materials

32oz (900g) of extra-bulky yarn
One pair No. 11 (7½mm) needles
2 buttons

Gauge

10 stitches to 4in (10cm) over garter stitch worked on No. 11 (7½mm) needles.

Back

Cast on 52 stitches.
Work 27½in (70cm) in garter stitch always slipping first stitch of every row. Bind off.

Front (make 2)

Cast on 26 stitches. Work as given for back.

To finish

☐ Darn in all ends of the yarn on one side of the knitting: this will be the wrong side.
☐ There is no need to press garter stitch —this will destroy the quality of the texture.
☐ With right sides of front and back together and bound-off edges matching, join top edges with a flat seam for 6¼in (16cm) from each side edge to form shoulder seams.
☐ Leave an 8in (20cm) gap for armholes, then join side seams with a flat seam to within 8in (20cm) of lower edge.
☐ On right side of work, turn back top corners of fronts to form triangles: sew on buttons to hold in place.

Caroline Arber

Mother and toddler's tops

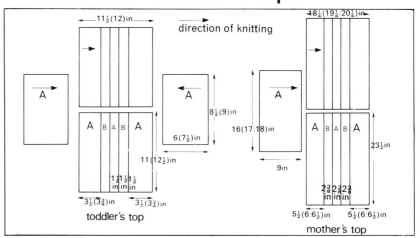

direction of knitting

toddler's top

mother's top

Sizes

These instructions are for the measurements shown on the diagrams.
Toddler's fits a 20[22]in (51[56]cm) chest.
Mother's is in small 32½/34in (83/87cm) bust, medium 34/36in (87/92cm) bust, and large 36/38in (92/97cm) bust sizes.
Note Directions for larger sizes are in brackets; where there is only one set of figures, it applies to all sizes.

Materials

Toddler's top:
4[6]oz (100[150]g) of a mohair-type yarn in color A
2oz (50g) of color B
One pair No. 10½ (7mm) needles

Mother's top:
9[11:13]oz (250[300:350]g) of color A
4oz (100g) of color B
One pair No. 10½ (7mm) needles

Gauge

14 stitches to 4in (10cm) over garter stitch worked on No. 10½ (7mm) needles.

Toddler's top

Back and front (alike)

☐ Using color A, cast on 39 [44] stitches for side edge.
☐ Work 3⅜in [3¾] in (8.5[9.5]cm) in garter stitch always slipping first stitch of every row. Note the number of rows you knit in this section: a row-counter is useful.
☐ Break off color A. Join color B and work 1½in (4cm) in garter stitch: work an even number of rows in each stripe, joining new yarn at same edge, so that the lines of broken stripes on changing color are on the wrong side.
☐ Break off color B. Work another 1½in (4cm) stripe in color A, then one in B.
☐ Join color A and work another 3⅜in [3¾] in (8.5[9.5]cm), knitting the same number of rows as in the previous section. Bind off loosely.

Sleeves (make 2)

☐ Use color A, cast on 28[32] stitches for cuff edge.
☐ Work 6[7½]in (15[19]cm) in garter stitch, always slipping first stitch of every row. Bind off loosely.

To finish

☐ Darn in all ends on the wrong side of the work. There is no need to press.
☐ With wrong sides of back and front together, join top edge with a flat seam for 3½[3¾]in (9[9.5]cm) from each side edge to form shoulder seams.
☐ Mark center of bound-off edge of sleeves with a pin. Open front and back sections out flat and with right sides facing, match pin to shoulder seams and pin bound-off edge along side edges of main piece. Sew with a backstitch seam.
☐ With right sides together, join side seams with a backstitch seam and sleeve seams with a flat seam, reversing seam for 1½in (4cm) at lower edge of sleeves (i.e. turn fabric so that wrong sides are together and sew seam on the right side of the work).
☐ Turn sweater right side out. Press seams lightly if necessary.
Fold back 1½in (4cm) at sleeve edges to form cuff.

Mother's top

Back and front (alike)

☐ Using color A, cast on 82[84:86] stitches for side edge.
☐ Work as for back and front of toddler's sweater, but following the measurements on the larger diagram.

Sleeves (make 2)

☐ Using color A, cast on 56[60:64] stitches for cuff edge. Work as for toddler's sleeves, but following the measurements on the larger diagram.

To finish

☐ Follow instructions for toddler's sweater, joining shoulder seams for 6[6¼:6¾]in (15[16:17]cm) from side edges and reversing sleeve seam for 2¾in (7cm) at the lower edge to form the cuff.

Knitting / COURSE 3

Move on to stockinette stitch

Working purl stitches

After learning how to knit stitches, you only need to know how to purl them to be able to construct an infinite number of fabrics and textures. A fabric made completely of purled stitches resembles garter stitch, and is not generally used: usually knit and purl stitches are combined to form a variety of fabrics.

Binding off purlwise

At some point in a pattern you may need to bind off on a purl row. Do this in exactly the same way as you bind off on a knit row, only purl the stitches before lifting one over another.

1 Hold the needle with the cast-on stitches in your left hand and the free needle in your right hand. Insert the free needle from right to left into the **front** of the stitch to be purled.

2 With the yarn at the front of the work throughout, wind it over and around the right-hand (RH) needle point.

3 Pull the yarn through the stitch on the left-hand (LH) needle to make a new loop on the RH needle.

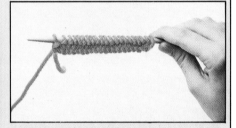

4 Drop the stitch from the LH needle and leave the new stitch on the RH needle. Work into each stitch to be purled in the same way.

Making a stockinette stitch fabric

With the second basic stitch, purl, you now know enough to knit in stockinette stitch, the most widely used knitted fabric. Originally it was used for knitted stockings; now it is found in many classic-style garments. Knit and purl rows alternate to produce a smooth-textured fabric. The right side of the work faces you when you are doing the knit rows. Since the stockinette stitch is easily reproduced by machine, it is often used for ready-made knitwear.

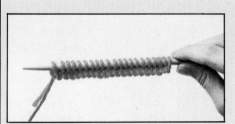

1 Take the needle with the cast-on stitches and knit each stitch in the first row.

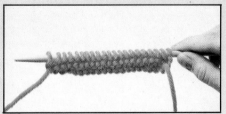

2 Purl each stitch in the second row: the wrong side of the fabric faces you.

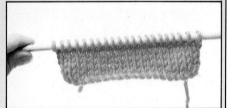

3 Knit one row, then purl one row alternately to produce a stockinette stitch fabric. The "right" side of the fabric has interlocking V shapes.

Paul Williams

Blocking and pressing a knitted fabric

Blocking is the method of pinning down pieces of knitting and pressing to give a correct shape and size. It is especially useful for stockinette stitch fabric because the edges tend to roll. The amount of pressing needed depends on the type of yarn used and directions are often given on the wrapper around the yarn.

1 Place knitting with wrong side up on a flat padded surface. If your ironing board is too small, improvise with folded blankets on a hard, flat surface such as the floor or a table top.

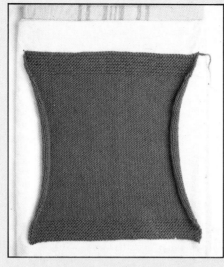

2 Ease piece into shape, then check measurements. Hold in position with plenty of pins. As you pin the knitting.

make sure that the stitches and rows run in straight lines and the fabric is not pulled out of shape.

3 Use a clean press cloth—slightly damp or dry according to the type of yarn. Many modern yarns need no pressing, but in general, press synthetics with a cool iron over a dry cloth, and natural fibers with a warm iron over a slightly damp cloth. Heavy pressing destroys the quality of many textured yarns and stitch patterns, such as garter stitch. Leave garter stitch borders free when pressing. Press evenly

and lightly, lifting and lowering the iron over the surface. Be sure that knitting is dry before taking out pins and lifting it up.

A sweater for all seasons

Our stockinette stitch sweater with garter stitch borders is made from simple pieces. It's a really versatile top that looks good over shirts or turtle-necks—or by itself!

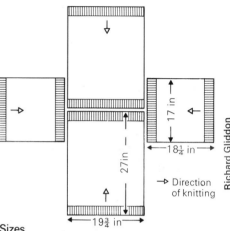

17 in

18¼ in

27 in

→ Direction of knitting

19¾ in

Sizes

These directions are for the measurements shown on the diagram: the sweater fits a range of bust sizes between 32½ and 36in (83—92cm).

Lengthen or shorten the sweater by working more (or less) stockinette stitch between the garter stitch borders on each piece. Remember that you may need more or less if you alter the length.

Materials

36oz (1000g) of a bulky yarn
One pair No. 10 (6½mm) needles

Gauge

15 stitches to 4in (10cm) in stockinette stitch worked on No. 10 (6½mm) needles.

To make sweater

Back

Cast on 72 stitches. Work 2½in (6cm) in garter stitch for border.

☐ Beginning with a knit row, continue in stockinette stitch until work measures 24½in (62cm) from cast-on edge, ending with a purl row.

☐ Work another 2½in (6cm) in garter stitch. Bind off loosely.

Front

Follow the directions for the back.

Sleeves (make 2)

Cast on 62 stitches. Work 2½in (6cm) in garter stitch for cuff.

☐ Beginning with a purl row, continue in stockinette stitch until work measures $15\frac{3}{4}$in (40cm) from cast-on edge, ending with a purl row.

☐ Work another $2\frac{1}{2}$in (6cm) in garter stitch. Bind off loosely.

To finish

Press each section, omitting garter stitch borders, according to type of yarn.

☐ With right sides of back and front and bound-off edges together join top edge with a backstitch seam for about $6\frac{3}{4}$in (17cm) from each side edge to form shoulder seams.

☐ Mark center of bound-off edge of sleeve with a pin.

☐ With right sides of knitting together, match center of sleeve top to shoulder seam and sew sleeve top in position with

backstitch seam.

☐ Again with right sides of knitting together and using a backstitch seam, join side and sleeve seams: if you want to turn back the garter stitch cuff, you must reverse the seam on this section by joining on the right side of the work.

☐ Press seams. Fold back cuffs.

Neil Kirk

*Using reverse stockinette stitch
*Picking up dropped stitches
*Pattern for a vest

Using reverse stockinette stitch

The wrong side of stockinette stitch—that is the side facing you as you purl a row—is a fabric in its own right. It has a densely looped texture in horizontal ridges which resembles garter stitch, but is less sculptured.

Work a classic-style garment in this fabric as a change from the more usual stockinette stitch: it is also a useful background for cable and Aran patterns.

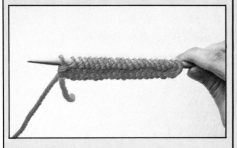

1 Always purl the first row of reverse stockinette stitch.

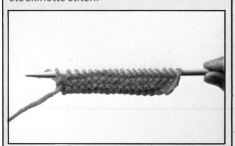

2 Alternate knit and purl rows exactly as in stockinette stitch. This is the right side of the fabric.

3 Note the finished piece of reverse stockinette stitch resembles garter stitch.

Picking up dropped stitches

Even experienced knitters drop stitches, so don't panic when it happens to you. One dropped stitch may be easy to cope with, but a number of stitches going down through the rows leave a "run" that is more of a problem. To prevent more

stitches from going farther, insert a safety pin from left to right to hold the stitches behind the "run" at the back of the work. You can now take the stitches one at a time and work them individually.

Method for garter stitch
Note If the stitch has dropped an even number of rows, follow the directions *in parentheses* below.

1 As the stitch unravels down through the rows it leaves horizontal strands of yarn.

2 With the horizontal strand of yarn lying across the front (back) of the stitch, insert the RH needle through the back (front) of the dropped stitch.

3 Push the RH needle from back (front) to front (back) under the horizontal strand of yarn.

4 Insert the left-hand needle through the back (front) of the dropped stitch.

5 Use the LH needle to lift the dropped stitch over the horizontal strand of yarn and off the needle.

6 The strand of yarn forms a stitch on the RH needle: transfer it to the correct knitting position on the LH needle by inserting the LH needle through the stitch back and withdrawing the RH needle.

Paul Williams

Method for stockinette stitch
Picking up a stitch on the right side

1 The unraveled stitches will leave horizontal strands of yarn.

2 On the right side of the knitting insert a crochet hook through the front of the loop at the bottom of the run pulling the lowest strand through to the front.

3 Work up the run in this way until you have the original stitch. Remove the crochet hook and replace the dropped stitch on the LH needle ready to be knitted. Make sure that the stitch is not twisted and that you work it as a knit stitch.

Picking up a stitch on the wrong side

1 Use a crochet hook, as before, to hook the bottom-most strand through the front of the lowest loop in the run.

2 Work up the run, but remove the crochet hook each time you move up to the next loop.

3 Replace the dropped stitch on the LH needle, making sure that it is not twisted, and work the stitch in purl.

Pretty casual vest

This little vest (see overleaf) is an invaluable addition to any wardrobe. The textured stripe effect is achieved by knitting bands of stockinette stitch and reverse stockinette stitch.

Sizes
These directions are for the measurements shown on the diagrams: the vest fits a woman with a $32\frac{1}{2}$in–34in (83–87cm) bust.
Lengthen or shorten the vest in multiples of 3in (8cm) by adding or subtracting a pattern repeat—$1\frac{1}{2}$in (4cm) stockinette stitch, $1\frac{1}{2}$in (4cm) reverse stockinette stitch—between the garter stitch borders at top and bottom.
Make the sections wider or narrower by casting on two stitches more or less for each $\frac{3}{8}$in (1cm) difference.
Remember that you need more or less yarn according to the size you make and whether you alter the length: in general allow approximately 1oz (25g) for each 2in (5cm) added to the bust size.

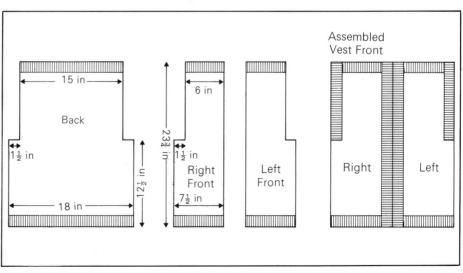

Materials
15oz (400g) of a sports yarn
One pair No. 5 (4mm) needles

Gauge
21 stitches and 30 rows to 4in (10cm)
in pattern on No. 5 (4mm) needles.

Back
Cast on 96 stitches for lower edge of back.
* Work 1½in (4cm) in garter stitch.
☐ Beginning with a knit row, work 1½in
(4cm) in stockinette stitch, ending with a
purl row.
☐ Beginning with a purl row, work 1½in
(4cm) in reverse stockinette stitch, ending
with a knit row.
☐ Repeat 3in (8cm) of pattern until back
measures 12½in (32cm) from cast-on
edge, ending with last row of a stockinette
stitch stripe. Stretch fabric open when
measuring as stripes of different textures
make a fabric fold up. *
☐ Bind off 8 stitches at the beginning of
the next 2 rows for armholes. 80 stitches
remain.
** Continue in the 3in (8cm) pattern
repeat until back measures 22in (56cm)
from cast-on edge, ending with last row of
a stockinette stitch stripe.
☐ Work 1½in (4cm) garter stitch for top
border. Bind off loosely to form top
edge. **

Left front
Cast on 40 stitches for lower edge. Make
in same way as back by repeating
directions in section marked at
beginning and end by an asterisk (*).
☐ Bind off 8 stitches at the beginning of
the next row for armhole. 32 stitches
remain.
☐ Now complete as given for the back by
repeating directions in section marked
by 2 asterisks (**).

Right front
Work as given for left front, but work 1
more row before the bind-off group for
armhole.

Borders
Cast on 9 stitches for one front border.
☐ Work in garter stitch, always slipping
the first stitch of each row to give a neat
edge, until border fits along front from
lower edge to top.
☐ Bind off loosely.
Make another border in the same way.
☐ Using the same number of stitches,
make two 22in (56cm) long strips of
garter stitch for armhole borders.

To finish
Block front and back sections as stripes of
stockinette stitch and reverse stockinette
stitch make a fabric fold up.
☐ Press, omitting garter stitch borders.
With right side of both fabrics together
and using a flat seam, sew front borders in

position: match cast-on edges of both
sections being sewn.
☐ With right side of both fabrics together
and using a backstitch seam, join bound-
off edges of fronts and back for about 4in
(10cm) from each side edge to form
shoulders.
☐ Fold armhole borders in half: with right

side of both fabrics together match center
of one edge of border to each shoulder
and using a flat seam, sew borders in
position.
☐ With right side of fabric together, use a
backstitch seam to join side seams.
☐ Turn vest right side out and lightly
press seams.

Neil Kirk

Working single ribbing

The use of both knit and purl stitches in the same row forms an elastic fabric called ribbing. Single ribbing is the most common of a number of ribbing patterns: it consists of knitting one stitch then purling one alternately across the first row. On subsequent rows each stitch that you knitted in the previous row is purled and each one that you purled is knitted.

The vertical "knit" ribs predominate, creating a stretchy fabric, which springs back into shape. It is ideal for the sections of a garment that need to grip, such as cuffs, waistbands and neckbands.

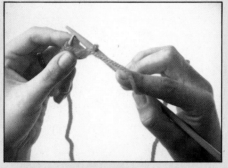

1 Cast on an even number of stitches. Knit the first stitch in the usual way; then take the yarn forward between the two needles so that it is at the front.

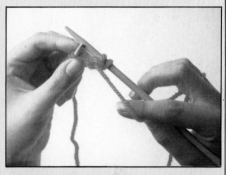

2 Purl the next stitch on the left-hand needle in the usual way.

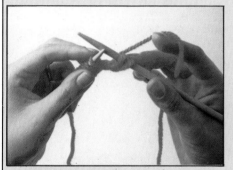

3 Take the yarn from the front to the back between the two needles.

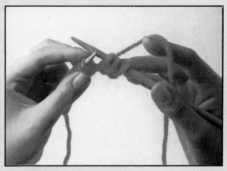

4 Knit the next stitch.

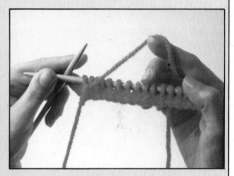

5 Continue in this way, alternately purling a stitch, then knitting a stitch, until the first row is complete, ending with a purled stitch.

6 Knit the first stitch on subsequent rows.

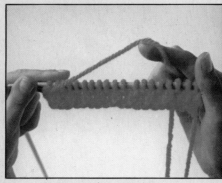

7 Work every row in the same knit and purl sequence.

8 Stretch the fabric slightly open to see that the knit stitches form raised vertical lines while the purl stitches recede.

Paul Williams

Binding off in ribbing

To retain the elasticity of any piece of ribbing you must bind off in ribbing: knit or purl the stitches in their correct sequence before lifting one stitch over another.

Don't press any ribbed fabric unless you are specifically told to do so: this again destroys its elastic qualities. Use a flat seam for joining ribbing, especially waistband or cuff sections on a garment.

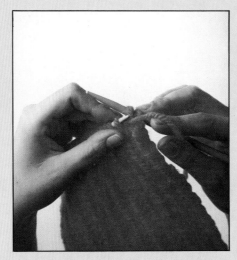

1 Keep ribbed pattern correct by knitting the first stitch on the left-hand needle and purling the second.

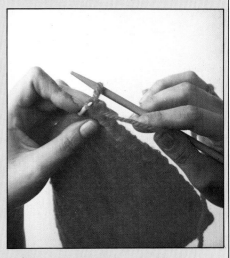

2 Use left-hand needle point to lift the first stitch over the second: keep the stitches fairly loose.

3 Knit the next stitch.

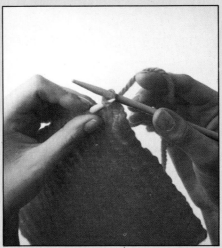

4 Bind off in the usual way

5 Purl the next stitch to keep ribbing sequence correct.

6 Bind off this stitch.

7 Continue in this way, alternating knit and purl.

8 The bound-off edge is as elastic as the main piece of knitting.

Paul Williams

Knitting / COURSE 6

Double ribbing

Altering the number of stitches in the knit and purl "ribs" adds variety to ribbed patterns. Double ribbing is a popular fabric, not quite as elastic as single ribbing, but with similar uses; it can also be used as an overall pattern for tight-fitting sweaters.

Double ribbing requires a multiple of four stitches plus two extra to make the pattern balance across the row. In the first row you knit two stitches and then purl two stitches alternately. The following rows are worked in the same way as single ribbing by knitting all purled stitches and purling all knitted stitches in the previous row.

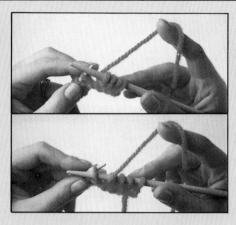

1 To make a sample piece of a double ribbing fabric, cast on any number of stitches that is a multiple of 4 (e.g. 12, 16, 20, 24) plus 2 extra stitches. For the **1st row** knit 2 stitches, then purl 2 stitches, continue in this way until you reach the last 2 stitches, knit 2.
2 To work the **2nd row** purl 2 stitches then knit 2 stitches, continue in this way until you reach the last 2 stitches, purl 2.

3 Repeat the 1st and 2nd rows for the length that you require, ending with a 2nd pattern row. Bind off in pattern, knitting or purling each stitch accordingly.
4 The finished fabric needs no blocking: it stretches slightly open when it is worn so that the vertical "ribs" are clearly visible.

Seed stitch

This is another simple variation of ribbing which produces a neat, overall pattern with a light "seeded" texture. Work the first row in the same way as single ribbing: on subsequent rows each stitch that you knitted in the previous row must be knitted again and each one that you purled must be purled again. Both sides of the fabric have the same appearance, so it is reversible.

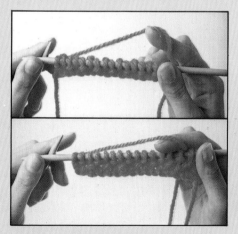

1 To make a sample cast on any even number of stitches (e.g. 16, 18, 20). For the **1st row** knit 1 stitch then purl 1 stitch, continue in this way until you reach the end of the row.
2 To work the **2nd row**, purl 1 stitch then knit 1 stitch, continue in this way until you reach the end of the row.

3 Repeat the 1st and 2nd rows for the length you need, ending with either row. Bind off in pattern, knitting or purling each stitch accordingly.
4 The finished fabric is flat, unlike ribbing. Block, pressing lightly if necessary, taking care not to flatten the texture.

Paul Williams

Basket stitch

Larger multiples of stitches and rows form blocks of stockinette stitch and reverse stockinette stitch in a familiar basket-weave pattern. You can make other fabrics by altering the number of stitches and rows in the blocks: remember that this may affect the multiple of stitches you cast on.

1 To make sample cast on any number of stitches that is a multiple of 8 (e.g. 16, 24, 32) plus 4 extra stitches. For the **1st row** knit 4 stitches then purl 4 stitches, continue in this way until you reach the last 4 stitches, knit 4.

2 To work the **2nd row** purl 4 stitches then knit 4 stitches, continue in this way until you reach the last 4 stitches, purl 4.

3 For the **3rd and 4th rows** repeat the directions for the 1st and 2nd rows.

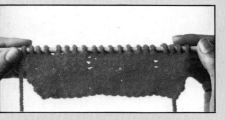

4 Alternate the blocks of pattern in the **5th to 8th rows** by repeating the 2nd, 1st, 2nd, 1st rows in that order.

5 Repeat these 8 rows for the length you need, ending with either pattern row 4 or 8. Bind off in pattern, knitting or purling each stitch accordingly.

6 The pattern is reversible: if necessary, block according to yarn used, pressing lightly.

Paul Williams

Baby's blanket

This bright, attractive crib blanket is fun to knit. Made from different-textured patches, it's an excellent way to practice simple stitch patterns.

Size
These directions are for the measurements shown on the diagram: the blanket is approximately 22 x 34in (56 x 84cm).

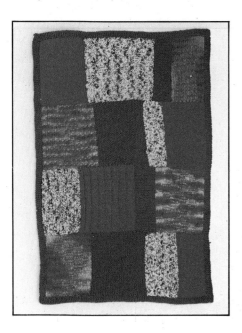

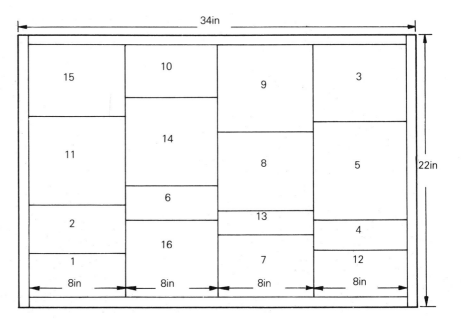

Materials

5oz (125g) of knitting worsted—
code A
4oz (100g) of bouclé tweed yarn—
code B
4oz (100g) of bouclé yarn—code C
3oz (75g) of mohair-type yarn—code D
One pair each Nos. 5, 7 and 9 (4, 5 and
6mm) knitting needles

To make blanket

The blanket consists of 16 pieces, which
all measure 8in (20cm) in length, but vary
in width. By numbering each individual
patch as it is completed, it will be easier to
put the blanket together when you have
finished knitting all the patches.

Patches 1-3 in stockinette stitch

No. 9 (6mm) needles and C, cast on 13.
No. 7 (5mm) needles and B, cast on 18.
No. 9 (6mm) needles and C, cast on 22.

Patches 4-6 are in garter stitch

No. 5 (4mm) needles and A, cast on 13.
No. 7 (5mm) needles and B, cast on 36.
No. 5 (4mm) needles and A, cast on 35.

Patches 7-9 are in seed stitch

No. 9 (6mm) needles and C, cast on 18.
No. 5 (4mm) needles and A, cast on 35.
No. 9 (6mm) needles and D, cast on 25.

Patches 10-12 are in single ribbing (K1, P1 rib)

No. 7 (5mm) needles and B, cast on 22.
No. 5 (4mm) needles and A, cast on 50.
No. 9 (6mm) needles and D, cast on 18.

Patches 13 and 14 are in double ribbing (K2, P2 rib)

No. 7 (5mm) needles and B, cast on 10.
No. 9 (6mm) needles and C, cast on 32.

Patches 15 and 16 are in basket stitch

No. 9 (6mm) needles and D, cast on 20.
No. 9 (6mm) needles and D, cast on 24.

Borders

Using No. 5 (4mm) needles and A, cast on
5 stitches.
Work 2 pieces in garter stitch each 32in
(80cm) long and another 2 pieces each
22in (56cm) long.

To finish

Darn in all ends on the wrong side of the
work. Only the sections in stockinette
stitch require blocking. Overcast the
patches together on the wrong side in
the order shown on the chart: make sure
that the knitting runs in the same direction
by having all cast-on edges at the same
edge of each strip.
Sew on the 2 long borders, then the 2
short ones.

George Wright

Bright braids

Weave pieces of braid and ribbon together to form a bright and colorful pillow cover.

Finished size
14in (35.5cm) square

Materials
$\frac{7}{8}$yd (.8m) of 36in (90cm)-wide solid cotton fabric
1yd (1m) pieces of 15 different braids and ribbons with a combined width of about 14in (36cm)
$1\frac{5}{8}$yd (1.4m) of filler cord or piping
14in (36cm) square pillow form
Matching sewing thread

1 From fabric cut out two pieces, each 15in (36cm) square, for back and front.
2 On center of pillow cover front, mark a 15in (36cm) square with basting stitches, the size of the pillow cover.
3 Cut each piece of braid and ribbon in half.
4 On pillow cover front, lay one piece of each braid and ribbon across the fabric. Arrange in an attractive order, placing the edges together and overlapping the basted lines at each side evenly.
5 Pin and baste both ends of each ribbon and braid in place along the basted lines on each side.
6 Weave the other piece of each braid and ribbon through the first set. Work over and under each piece in the same order as before.
7 Pin and baste in place as described in step 5.
8 Stitch around the pillow front on the basted lines.
9 For cording cut out 2in (5cm)-wide strips on the bias from remaining fabric. Pin, baste and stitch the strips together with bias seams to make a strip 59in long
10 Fold cording fabric evenly around the filler cord, with wrong sides inside. Pin and baste close to the cord. Or use ready-made piping if you prefer.
11 With cording facing inward, pin, baste and stitch filler cord to pillow front on basted line, joining ends of piping fabric and cord together so that they fit.
12 Position back on front, right sides together, matching outer edges. Pin, baste and stitch all around on basted line, leaving a 10in (25cm) opening on one side.
13 Trim seams and clip diagonally across the corners. Turn right side out.
14 Insert pillow form through opening. Turn in opening edges. Slip stitch folded edges together to close.

Sewing

Step-by-step course—1
Equipment and fabrics

*Sewing machines
*Basic dressmaking kit
*Choosing needles and threads
*Know your fabric
*Best fabrics for beginners

Sewing machines

A sewing machine is the most important and expensive piece of equipment you need. Many people already have a machine or access to one, but it's worth knowing about the main types now on the market. All of them are suitable for light dressmaking and household sewing, but if you plan to do any tailoring, you should avoid the fully automatic machine.

Straight-stitch type: sews only with a straight-stitch; most will sew in reverse as well; ask what extra attachments are available; lowest price bracket: varies according to quality and make.

Zig-zag type: does zig-zag and straight-stitching; useful for finishing raw edges, insertions, appliqués and buttonholes; some have automatic buttonhole reverse and most come with a good range of attachments; medium price range; re-commended as the most useful and economical for the home dressmaker.

Automatic zig-zag type: all the facilities of the straight-stitch and zig-zag machine, and embroiders automatically; you can create a wide range of effects by inserting special discs or using automatic settings; most expensive type; a luxury item unless you plan to do a lot of decorative stitching and embroidery.

Basic dressmakers' kit

These items will take you through from the simplest dressmaking to more advanced work.

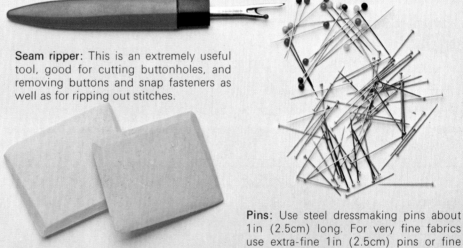

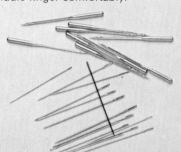

Tape measure: Buy a fiberglass one that doesn't stretch. Replace it when it gets worn.

Thimble: Essential for neat, accurate hand stitching, to help hold the needle at the correct angle and to protect your fingers. Buy a metal one that fits your middle finger comfortably.

Seam ripper: This is an extremely useful tool, good for cutting buttonholes, and removing buttons and snap fasteners as well as for ripping out stitches.

Tailor's chalk: For marking important points on your cut-out fabric pieces; light shade for dark fabrics, dark shade for light fabrics.

Pins: Use steel dressmaking pins about 1in (2.5cm) long. For very fine fabrics use extra-fine 1in (2.5cm) pins or fine sewing needles to avoid marking the fabric. Color ball pins are usually used for lace and net fabrics—they may break if you machine-stitch over them.

Needles: It is important to get the right sewing and machine needles for the fabric you are stitching. The chart on the next page gives you a guide. Remember to check the sharpness of needles occasionally—and change them if necessary. A blunt needle in the sewing machine can damage the fabric by dragging the threads; it will skip stitches and can also damage the machine.

Scissors: Ideally you should have three pairs. Bent-handle dressmaker shears 7 or 8in (18 or 20cm) long are essential; one pair of small sewing scissors about 5in (12.5cm) and a pair of embroidery scissors are useful as well. Try to buy the best rust-proof ones.

Yardstick: used for measuring hems and connecting points for straight seams.

Iron: Pressing is a vital part of dress-making. A good medium-weight iron with temperature controls is essential. Be sure to keep the base clean. An ironing board with a smooth-fitting cover is necessary, and you will find a small sleeve board very useful too. A piece of muslin or a press cloth is needed for steam pressing.

Paul Williams

Dressmaking threads

These are the types you are likely to need in home dressmaking.

Basting thread: loosely twisted cotton thread that breaks easily. Comes in white only.

Mercerized cotton: for cottons and general sewing.

Heavy-duty mercerized cotton: for heavy fabrics such as denim.

Synthetic thread: for synthetic fabrics and blends, knits and heavy woolens.

Pure silk: for very fine fabrics such as chiffon, voile, silk and for knits and light woolens.

Buttonhole twist: thicker than ordinary sewing thread, made of pure silk or a synthetic; for hand-stitched buttonholes and top stitching.

You will find that most synthetic threads are unnumbered, but natural threads usually have a number on the spool. With all types, the higher the number, the finer the thread. See the chart on this page for a guide to which thread suits each kind of fabric.

Needle and thread numbers at a glance

Fabric	Thread	Machine Needle Sizes	Hand Sewing Needles
Very fine Voile Chiffon	mercerized cotton—70, 100 silk synthetic	size 9	sharps—sizes 10, 11 embroidery—size 9
Fine lawn Fine cotton Silk	mercerized cotton—60, 70 silk synthetic	sizes 9-11	sharps—size 9 embroidery—size 8
Medium weight (for general sewing)	mercerized cotton—40, 50, 60 silk synthetic	sizes 9-11	sharps—sizes 7, 8 embroidery—sizes 6, 7
Heavyweight Velours Tweeds	mercerized cotton—40 silk synthetic	sizes 11-16	sharps—sizes 6-8 embroidery—size 6
Jersey	mercerized cotton—60, 70 silk synthetic	sizes 9-11 (ball point)	sharps—sizes 8, 9 embroidery—sizes 7, 8
Leather	heavy-duty mercerized cotton—8, 16, 20 button and carpet thread	sizes 16-18	sharps—sizes 6-8 embroidery—sizes 3-5

The best fabrics for beginners

While learning new techniques and putting them into practice, it is best to avoid using difficult-to-handle fabrics. A fabric composed of natural fibers—cotton or wool—or a blend of natural and synthetic fibers is the best choice for the inexperienced dressmaker. These fabrics are the easiest to handle since they are least likely to ravel while you are working on them. The fabric types illustrated on this page are all suitable.

☐ If the fabric is cotton, choose a small or medium overall print so that you do not have to think about matching patterns or deal with one-way designs. For woolens choose a closely woven fabric in a tweedy mixture or a small check, which will not need to be matched.

☐ Until you are more experienced avoid working on plain fabrics, which tend to show up every mistake or any ripping out that may need to be done. Also avoid jersey, velvet or silky, slippery fabrics and those which ravel or wrinkle easily.

Cotton shirting
Printed cotton lawn
Crinkle cotton
Cotton print
Cotton print
Cotton/polyester gauze
Woven cotton seersucker
Cotton print
Lightweight polyester/cotton denim
Dressweight printed wool challis
Woven check Viyella®
Dressweight flecked tweed
Harris tweed

David Levin

Know your fabric

You will come across three important terms in dressmaking, which between them explain how a woven fabric is constructed.

Grain: There is a lengthwise and crosswise "grain" to a fabric; usually a pattern piece will need to be positioned in relation to this. The warp threads running down the length of the fabric indicate lengthwise grain; the weft threads running across indicate the crosswise grain. In some printed fabrics you may find the pattern does not run true to the grain. When this happens, work to the grain on small prints, but follow the pattern on larger prints.

Selvage: This is the narrow, flat, woven border at each edge of the fabric. The lengthwise grain runs parallel to the selvage.

Bias: The bias is a diagonal intersecting the weft and warp threads. Fabric cut on the bias is very stretchy, and sometimes a pattern piece will be cut on the bias to take advantage of this. Find the bias by folding the fabric diagonally, with the weft threads parallel to the selvage.

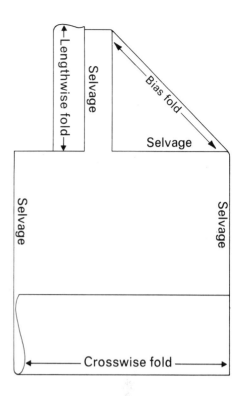

Straightening fabric before cutting out

1 If the fabric has been wrinkled on the bolt, press it before cutting out.

2 Trim each cut edge so that it is precisely at right angles to the selvage. If the fabric has a horizontal stripe or pattern, follow that as a guide. For cotton and linen-type fabrics, pull a thread across the width as a guide.

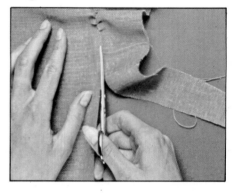

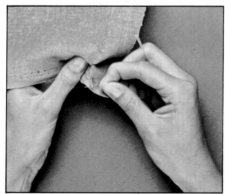

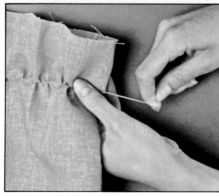

3 On fabrics where it is difficult to pull a thread, line up a right-angled triangle with the selvage, and mark the horizontal with tailor's chalk.

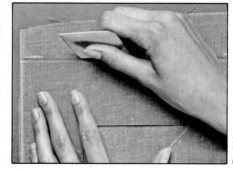

David Levin

4 After trimming the ends, place your selvages together and adjust the fabric until it lies flat.

5 Press out the central foldline unless you are using the fabric folded exactly that way in your cutting layout.

*Correct machine stitch
*The stitch length
*Plain seam
*Finishing raw edges
*Simple hem

Correct machine stitch

The tension controls

For a good end result, you need to know how to get the right tension and stitch size for the fabric' you are sewing. Before you start on a garment, test this on a scrap of the fabric used double.

Unless you want to create a special effect, such as top stitching, make sure you have the same *type* of thread in the bobbin and on top of the machine, or the tension will be affected. (The bobbin is the spool enclosed in a metal case underneath the stitching plate; the lower thread feeds up from the bobbin.)

When testing the tension, however, it makes it easier to use a different color thread on top of the machine from that in the bobbin, so that you can identify which may be too tight or too loose.

Whichever tension is wrong, it should usually be possible to correct it by adjusting the top tension spring. Avoid altering the bobbin tension unless all else fails. A few new models have automatic pre-set tension which needs no adjustment.

The top thread feed control governs the tension of the thread that goes through the needle. On most machines it is a dial on the front of the tension spring numbered 0-9. Turn the dial to adjust the tension; the higher the number, the tighter the feed.

To adjust the bobbin tension on the machine, slightly loosen or tighten the tiny screw on the bobbin case that holds down the steel clip.

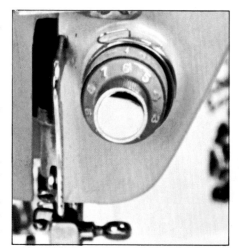

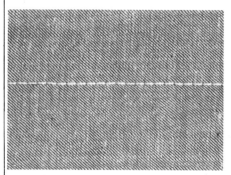
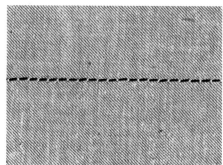
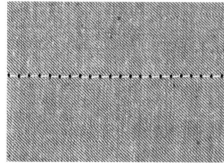

Correct tension. The stitching on the top and underside should look identical, with the upper and lower threads drawn into the center of the fabric to the same degree.

Top tension too loose. The stitching on the underside looks flat. Adjust tension spring to higher number until correct.

Top tension too tight. The stitching on the top looks flat. Adjust tension spring to lower number until correct.

The stitch length

The weight and texture of the fabric determine the stitch length, but generally, delicate fabrics require a shorter, finer stitch than heavy fabrics. This table gives you a specific guide.

The stitch length control in older models is usually a screw-knob which adjusts vertically; in newer machines it is usually a dial.

Fabric	Very fine chiffon, voile	Fine lawn, fine cotton, silk	Medium weight (for general sewing)	Heavy weight velours, tweeds	Jersey	Leather
Number of machine stitches per inch	16	12–14	10–14	8–12	14–16	6–8

Plain seam

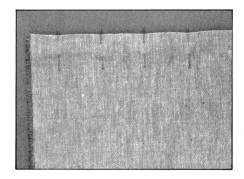

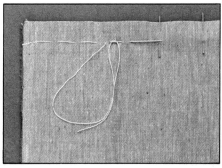

1 Line up your two pieces of fabric, checking that right sides are together and the edges even. Insert the pins at right angles to the outer or raw edges, placing them exactly on the stitching line, about 2in (5cm) apart.

2 Baste along stitching line. Anchor the thread at the beginning with a double backstitch and work along the seam, using stitches about $\frac{3}{8}$in (1cm) long and $\frac{1}{4}$in (6mm) apart. Secure the thread at the end with a double backstitch. Remove pins.

3 Machine stitch the seam using the basting stitches as a guide to keep it smooth and even. Stitch slightly to one side of the basting, not right on top of it.

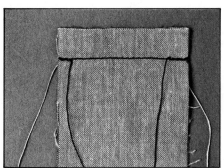

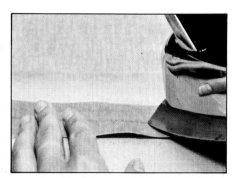

4 Finish off the ends with a knot: make a loop over a pin and slide the knot along to the edge of the fabric.

5 If your machine can reverse stitch, secure the ends by starting $\frac{3}{8}$in (1cm) in from the edge, reverse stitching to the edge and then stitching forward to complete the seam. Stitch to within a fraction of the end and reverse stitch for $\frac{3}{8}$in (1cm).

6 Press on the reverse side inserting strips of brown paper under the seam allowance to avoid leaving a ridge on the right side of the garment. Open up the seam using just the tip of the iron, and move the iron along the stitching line in the direction that the seam was stitched.

Finishing raw edges

To prevent raveling, and give a professional look inside a garment, it is essential to finish the raw edges of a seam. Finish the seams as you make them, using one of these methods.

Straight machine stitch method: recommended for fine to medium-weight cotton such as poplin and wool/cotton blends such as Viyella®. It would create too much bulk if used on thick denim or tweed fabric.

With the wrong side of the fabric facing up, turn under about $\frac{1}{8}$in (3mm) on the raw edge and machine stitch.

Zig-zag stitch method: suitable for most fabrics except some lightweight silks, where it might show through to the right side of the garment. If working on fine fabrics such as voile, use silk thread for a finer finish.

Set the machine to zig-zag stitch and test on a piece of fabric, adjusting the length and width of the stitch to give a neat finish without any puckering or rolling of the edge. The position of the fabric under the needle is very important, to avoid "chewing" the edge of the fabric. On fabrics that fray, trim the raveled edge back close to the stitching.

David Levin   Paul Williams

Simple hem

This hem is suitable for fine to medium-weight cottons, wool/cotton blends, and cotton/synthetic blends.

Because of variations in figure types, trying on the garment is the only way to get an even hemline. Stand straight wearing shoes the height you are likely to wear with the garment. If you haven't anyone to help, trial and error—trying on, pinning and re-pinning—is the only way.

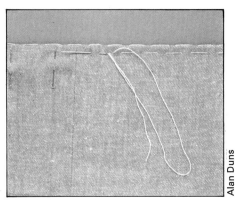

Alan Duns

1 Mark hem level, using yardstick and chalk or pins. If the chalk won't mark the fabric clearly or pins do not hold, mark the hemline immediately with a line of basting stitches.

2 Turn up the hem on the line you have marked and baste close to the foldline.

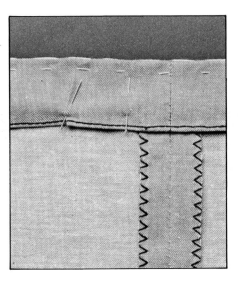

3 Mark desired hem depth all around—anything from 1 to $2\frac{1}{2}$in (2.5-6cm) is suitable.

4 Fold extra fabric to wrong side along this line and machine stitch close to folded edge. Trim extra fabric close to line of stitching.

5 Matching seamlines, pin and baste the hem to the garment. Make tiny tucks where necessary to remove any fullness.

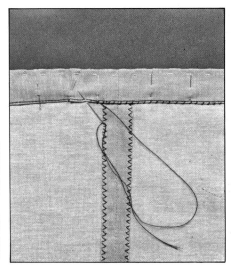

David Levin Paul Williams

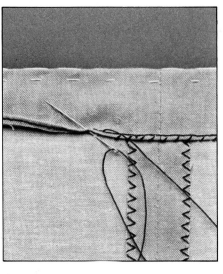

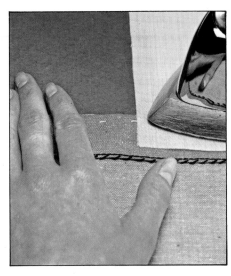

6 Sew the hem to the garment by hand, using hemming stitch. Make stitches at $\frac{1}{4}$in (6mm) intervals as shown.

7 To work **hemming stitch**, start by making a double backstitch on hem allowance edge, then pick up alternately one thread of the fabric and a tiny piece of the hem edge.

8 Press the hem flat, pressing the edge only. Do not press the hem stitch.

Sewing / COURSE 3

Basic techniques for Paper Patterns

This unit of the course gives you the basic techniques you need to use our Stitch by Stitch Sewing Patterns, but you will find the information equally helpful in using a purchased commercial pattern.

Using cutting layouts

A cutting layout shows you exactly how to position and cut out the pieces of a pattern from a given amount of fabric; there will be cutting layouts to cover each fabric width.

The layout is planned to allow the pattern to be cut from the least amount of fabric. If you find you have a lot of fabric left over after pinning on the pattern pieces, check to ensure that each piece is aligned as indicated on the piece with the true grain of the fabric. If parts of the garment are cut slightly off-grain the hang of the garment will be affected.

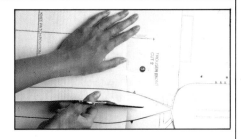

1 Consult the list of pattern pieces in the directions for the garment. If the pieces are printed together on a large sheet, cut the pieces you need from the sheet.

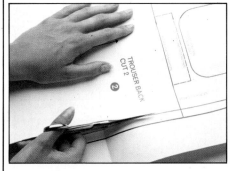

2 For multi-size patterns, such as those in Stitch by Stitch, select your size and cut around the line indicated on each pattern piece.

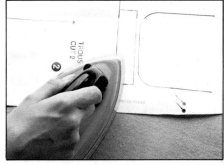

3 If the paper pieces are very creased, press them flat with a cool iron.

4 Prepare and fold your fabric, following the cutting layout. If you are working with the fabric doubled, fold it with right sides together. For single fabric work with the wrong side up.

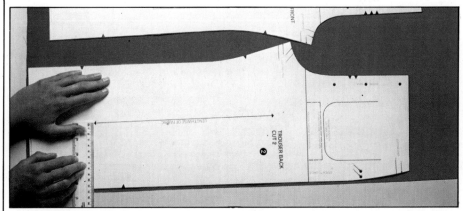

5 Lay the pattern pieces on the fabric, following the cutting layout for the width of fabric you are using.
If the fabric you are using has a pile (i.e. corduroy or velvet), or a one-way design, check to make sure your pattern pieces are all running in the same direction on the fabric, from top to bottom.
Check that the straight grain mark on every pattern piece runs parallel to the selvages; if a pattern piece is marked "to be positioned on the bias" check that it is laid on the fabric at the correct angle.

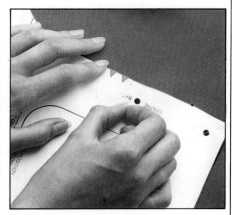

6 Pin the pattern to the fabric, placing the pins about 2in (6cm) apart, pointing toward the outer edges. This gives the firmest hold. Keep pins within seam allowances to avoid marking.

Paul Williams

Cutting out

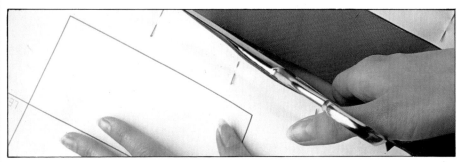

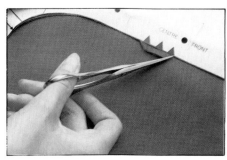

1 Following the cutting line, cut out your pattern pieces, making sure you cut through both thicknesses of fabric if you are using your material double. Use large dressmaking shears for the long, straight edges; when you come to an awkward corner, it is easier to use a small pointed pair.

2 Wherever you see notches marked, either singly or in groups, use the smaller scissors to cut around them. These notches are important markings for making up the garment properly. Do not cut *into* the notches; this weakens and lessens the seam allowance.

Transferring pattern markings

You will see various circles and dotted lines marked on your pieces. These indicate points where darts or pleats will be made, where a waistband or cuff is to be matched to another piece, where pockets or facings are to be applied, etc. Whatever their purpose, these markings are important; you need to transfer them before you start putting the garment together.

There are many different techniques and devices for transferring these markings to your fabric. Tailor's tacks, tailor's chalk and dressmaker's carbon paper should give you enough choice for most fabrics and patterns.

Making tailor's tacks
Suitable for all fabrics. Use to mark darts, circles, button positions, pocket positions.

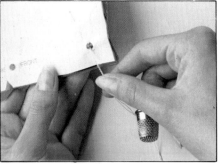

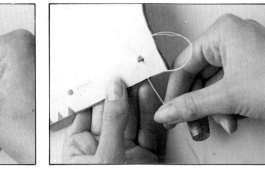

1 Thread a needle with a long double thread in contrasting color to fabric.

2 Work a small stitch through the pattern and both thicknesses of material, leaving about 1in (2.5cm) of thread free.

3 Work another stitch in the same place leaving a loop of thread about 1½in (4cm) long.

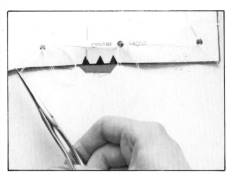

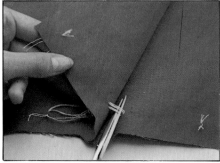

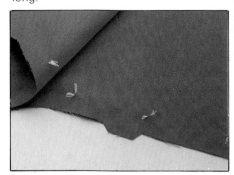

4 Tailor's tacks can be worked in groups— leave large loops between stitches and clip them when you are finished. Cut the thread 1in (2.5cm) from the last stitch.

5 Clip each loop. Remove the paper pattern piece. Pull the two pieces of fabric apart very gently and clip the threads in between, to form tufts.

6 Both pieces of fabric are now clearly marked with a row of tailor's tacks.

Paul Williams

Tailor's chalk or marking pencil

These are the quickest and simplest methods of marking, but you must test on a scrap of fabric first to check that the marking will show clearly. If it doesn't, use tailor's tacks instead.

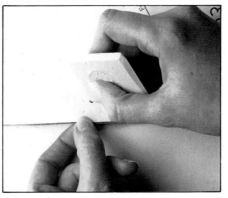

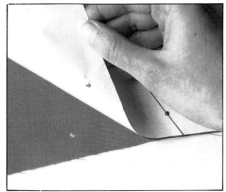

1 Make a pin hole in point to be marked.

2 Mark fabric with chalk through the pin hole.

3 Unpin pattern pieces and re-pin to other side. Repeat marking process.

Dressmaker's carbon paper

Good for light, smooth fabrics but unsuitable for nubby tweeds. Make *sure* you are marking on the *wrong* side of your fabric.

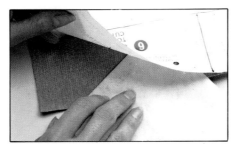

1 Work by unpinning a small area of a pattern at a time. Slide the carbon paper between the pattern and the fabric where markings need to be made.

2 Trace over the markings with a pencil or tracing wheel, being careful not to tear the pattern.

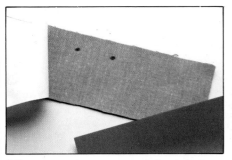

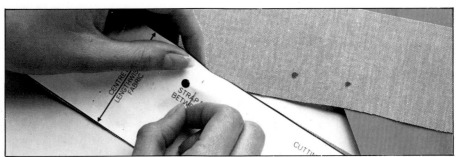

3 Remove carbon paper and check that markings have transferred. Complete all markings for that pattern piece. Re-pin area and move on.

4 If working a double fabric, complete one set of markings then separate the pieces of fabric and re-pin the paper pattern to the wrong side of the underneath piece. Transfer markings as before.

Marking seam allowances

Beside circles and dotted line markings, you may wish to mark a seam allowance. Unless otherwise stated, this is $\frac{5}{8}$in (1.5cm) on all Stitch by Stitch patterns. First remove the paper pattern, then measure allowance and mark with ordinary basting or tailor's chalk.

Once you get used to gauging a seam allowance this will be unnecessary. Also, many modern machines have markings on the plate under the needle which show you exactly where to line up your fabric to stitch $\frac{5}{8}$in (1.5cm) in from the edge.

Paul Williams

Patch pockets

Patch pockets can be cut in practically any shape desired, in matching or contrasting fabric. Although they are the simplest form of pocket to make, they nevertheless need great care in making and applying, since they usually form a focal point on the garment.

If you are really inexperienced, it is advisable to practice making and applying them with some extra fabric until you are completely satisfied with the end result, before using them on a garment.

The method can vary, depending on the shape and type of pocket. The techniques described here are for making a basic square or rectangular patch pocket. The method is particularly suitable for use on garments made in medium-weight fabrics. Corduroy, denim and sailcloth are all good fabrics for patch pockets.

The position of pockets is very important. For instance a pocket at bust level can look very unattractive if it is badly placed, and the proportion of a dress can be ruined if the pockets are placed too high or too low to suit individual figures. If the pocket is to be "used," rather than serve just for decorative effect, it must be easily accessible to the hand; the hand should be able to reach inside to the bottom.

For striped, checked or printed fabrics, the pockets must be cut to correspond with the area which they are to be attached so that the pattern is not broken or interrupted. Therefore, when using patterned fabrics, do not cut out the pockets before you have tested for positioning, so that you can carefully match up any pattern on both the garment and the pocket.

Checking pocket position

1 Cut out pockets in paper and trim off the seam and facing allowance.

2 Pin the paper pockets to the placing line marked on the garment section.

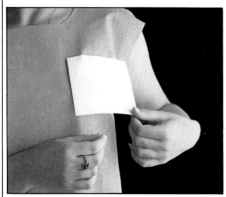

3 Hold the garment section against the figure and, looking in a mirror, adjust pocket position if necessary.

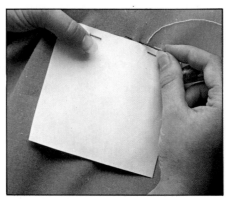

4 Mark new position line with basting before unpinning paper pocket.

Making the pocket

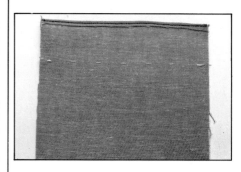

1 On the upper edge of the pocket, which forms the facing, finish the raw edge by turning $\frac{1}{8}$in (3mm) to the wrong side of the fabric and machine stitching.

3 To reduce bulk and ensure sharp point, at the corners, cut off the corners of the seam allowance. To avoid cutting into the stitching, cut *away* from the top of the stitching at an angle.

5 With the right side of the pocket facing you, baste close to the folded edge at the top of the pocket.

Attaching pocket to garment

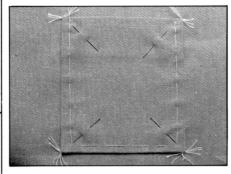

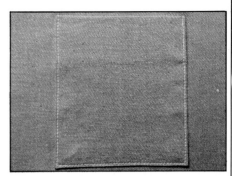

1 With the wrong side of the pocket placed on the right side of the garment, pin and baste it in place according to the positioning line. The pocket must lie perfectly flat on the garment.

2 Sew the pocket to the garment using machine topstitching $\frac{1}{8}-\frac{1}{4}$in (3-6mm) away from the pocket edge, being careful to follow any curve smoothly.

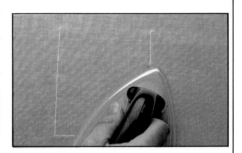

3 Reinforce stitching at upper edges by reverse stitching twice at the beginning and end of the seam.
If you cannot reverse, reinforce by taking the thread ends to the back of the work. Thread them in a needle and work several backstitches through to the pocket, but invisible on the right side.

4 Press the pocket flat on the wrong side. Avoid pressing on the right side—this may create "shine" on the edges of the pocket.

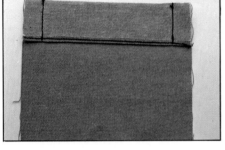

2 With the right sides together, fold the pocket on the foldline. Baste and stitch the facing short seams.

4 Turn the pocket right side out and gently poke the corners into good points with a knitting needle.

6 Turn in the seam allowance around the side and lower edges of the pocket, being careful to ease any curve into a good shape as you do so. Press the pocket flat. Baste outer edges.

Functional topstitching

The techniques used to create decorative topstitching will be covered in another course. Here we explain how to work functional topstitching, which is used to give extra strength to a seam or hem, or as part of the garment construction.

Topstitching is worked from the right side of the garment at a predetermined distance from the edge of garment pieces or from the seamline. The distance can vary from $\frac{1}{8}-\frac{1}{4}$in (3—6mm). Most sewing machines have a foot that you can use as a guide for the $\frac{1}{8}$in (3mm) stitching. If not you will have to mark or judge the distance for yourself. For the $\frac{1}{4}$in (6mm) distance, you can judge the distance by stitching the width of the machine foot away from the edge or line to be topstitched.

In many cases, it is best to baste along the topstitching line first. This gives you a much clearer guide to follow when you are stitching, and controls the fabric at the same time.

1 Thoroughly press the sections to be topstitched.

2 Baste along the line to be topstitched.

3 Topstitch close to the basting. Remove basting and finish off ends securely.

Paul Williams

55

*Using bias strips
*Facing a slashed opening
*Gathering
*Pattern for a raglan-sleeved blouse: directions for making (1)

Using bias strips

Bias strips cut from the same or contrasting fabric, are widely used in dressmaking; because they are cut on the bias they have an elastic quality which makes them perfect for a number of techniques. They are used for binding raw edges and making tubing, but they can also be used for a variety of decorative purposes.

Ready-cut and folded bias binding can be purchased. This is suitable for some exterior trims, and is also useful for finishing awkward seams inside a garment. A pattern should state whether ready-made binding is a suitable alternative to a self-fabric bias strip.

Cutting bias strips

Bias strips can be cut to varying widths depending on use. To determine how wide to cut the strip, first decide how deep you want the finished binding to be. Double this measurement and add another $\frac{1}{4}$in (6mm) to each raw edge for seam allowance.

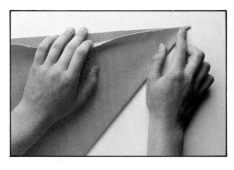

1 Check to find the true bias of the fabric, and mark the line of the bias with chalk or a basting thread.

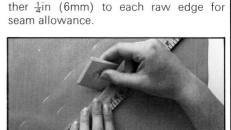

2 Using tailor's chalk and a yardstick, measure and mark the strips accurately. Cut out.

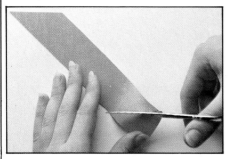

3 If the strips are to be joined to make a long piece, trim all the ends on the straight grain.

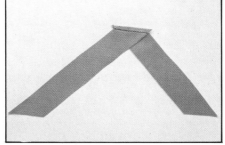

4 To join the strips place two strips right sides together and at right angles to each other. Stitch seam $\frac{1}{4}$in (6mm) in from raw edges.

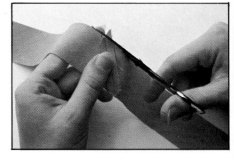

5 Press seam open and cut off corners.

Binding an edge with bias strips

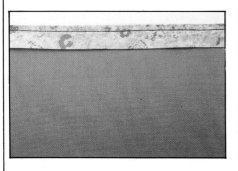

1 With right sides together and with the seamline of the binding placed to the seamline of the garment, pin, baste and stitch the binding to the garment edge.

2 On the right side, press the binding away from the garment.

3 On the inside, turn under the seam allowance on the binding and press.

Paul Williams

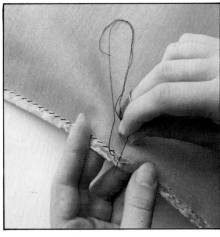

4 Baste the folded edge close to the row of machine stitching, on the inside of the garment.

5 Hem the folded edge of the binding to the line of stitching.

6 Press flat on wrong side.

Making tubing from bias strips

Tiny "tubes" of fabric made from bias strips are frequently used to make ties and button loops and can also be used as a decorative trim.

The secret of making a well-rounded, self-filled tube is to leave sufficient seam allowance to fill it without making it too stiff. When cutting the strips of fabric make them six times the width of the finished tube. For example, to create a $\frac{1}{4}$in (6mm)-wide tube, cut a strip $1\frac{1}{2}$in (3cm) wide. Make the strip four times the finished width if you are using a thick fabric. The seam needs elasticity, so use a short stitch with a slight zig-zag.

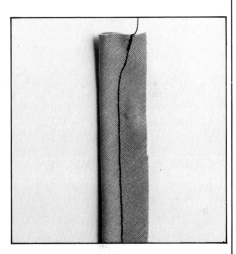

1 Cut a bias strip to width required. Join, if necessary, to form length required.

2 With right sides together, having raw edges even, fold the strips in half lengthwise, baste and stitch $\frac{1}{4}$in (6mm) from folded edge, finishing the stitching by widening it slightly at one end, leaving long ends of thread.

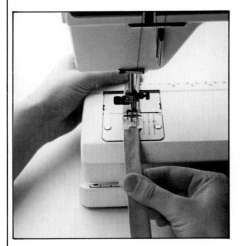

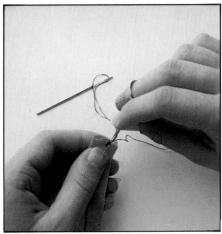

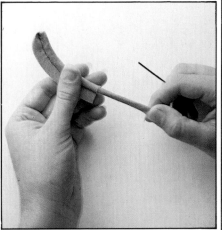

3 If your machine does not zig-zag, then stretch the fabric slightly as you machine stitch.

4 Thread the ends of the sewing thread into a bodkin and secure ends with a double backstitch.

5 Thread the bodkin or needle through the tubing and pull the tube right side out.

Paul Williams

Facing a slashed opening (on neck or sleeve)

This type of facing is made without an interfacing. It is particularly useful on fine fabrics where an interfacing would be too stiff or might show through to the right side of the garment. Adding a facing of this type is a very quick and simple way to finish a sleeve opening.

If you want to apply this facing to a garment that has no pattern piece for it, you can cut your own very easily. For a sleeve opening cut a rectangle 1¾in (4.5cm) longer than the opening by 3in (7.5cm) wide. For a neck opening cut it 2¾in (7cm) longer and 5½in (14cm) wide.

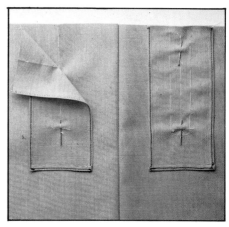

1 To finish the outer edge of the facing, turn under ⅛in (3mm) along the two long edges and across one short end and machine stitch. Press.

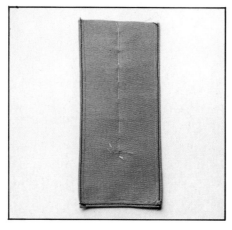

2 With right sides together, pin and baste the facing to the garment with the center of the facing placed along the slash marking for the opening.

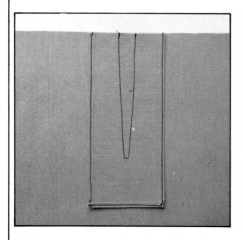

3 Stitch along both sides of marking, starting ¼in (6mm) from the edge, tapering to a point. Take an extra two stitches across the point to ensure a sharp corner when turned.

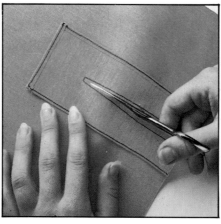

4 Slash between stitching to the point and turn the facing to wrong side.

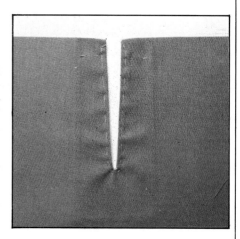

5 On the right side, baste close to seam edge, easing into shape. Press on wrong side.

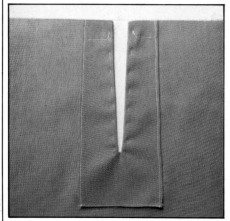

6 Baste the loose ends of the facing to the outer edge with raw edges even.

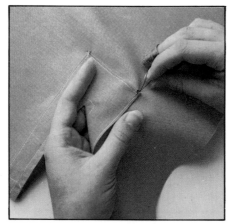

7 If desired, catch the corners of the facing to the garment with three or four stitches. The stitches should not show on the right side.

8 Topstitching around the opening edge helps to hold the facing back. Topstitch along both sides and across the bottom of the opening ⅛ or ¼in (3 or 6mm) in from edges. Press.

Paul Williams

Gathering

Gathering is a method used to control fullness. It can be used on any part of the garment where the design dictates— at sleeve edges and cuffs or where bodice meets yoke or waist or where skirt is gathered into a waistband.

Directions often say "run a row of gathering stitches." This does not mean one row of stitching—it means two. Two rows are essential to control the fullness correctly.

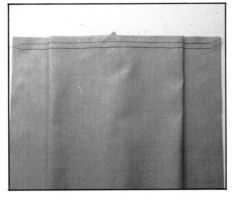

1 Adjust machine to the longest stitch. Run one row of stitching $\frac{1}{8}$in (3mm) below the seamline and another row $\frac{1}{8}$in (3mm) above the seamline, leaving long ends to pull up the gathering.

2 On the wrong side, working from each edge alternately, pick up the two loose ends at one edge of the work and pull them while holding the fabric in the other hand. Pull the gathers to the approximate length desired.

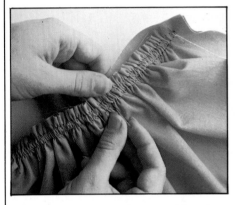

3 With right sides together, matching any circles and notches, pin the gathered edge to the straight edge of fabric, inserting the pins at right angles to the edge.

4 Adjust the length of the gathering threads until the gathered edge fits the straight one.

5 Using a pin, distribute the gathers until they are evenly spaced, but keep notches and circles matched. Re-pin with the pins spaced as little as $\frac{1}{4}$in (6mm) apart if necessary to hold the gathers firmly in place.

6 Baste the seam, but do not remove the pins, which help hold and control the gathers while stitching.

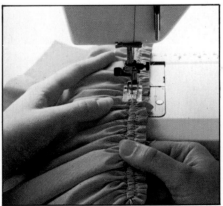

7 With the gathered side upward, stitch the seam on the seamline between the two rows of gathering stitches. Stitch slowly and evenly, being careful not to hit the pins with the machine needle. Change the needle after completing the garment; it will be blunted by stitching over the pins.

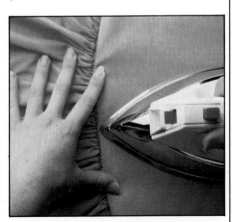

8 Press the seam away from the gathers, but do not press the gathers themselves.

Paul Williams

Raglan blouse:
directions for making (1)

This versatile and pretty blouse is easy to make. Soft easing and raglan sleeves make it a flattering shape for all figures. The directions for making it are divided into two separate parts and are completed in the next Course.

Measurements
The pattern is given in sizes 10, 12, 14, 16, 18 and 20; corresponding to sizes 8 to 18 in ready-made clothes.

Suggested fabrics
Soft cottons, wool/cotton blends or cotton/synthetic blends. For more experienced dressmakers: fine wool, cotton or synthetic knits, silk or synthetics.

Materials
36in (90cm)-wide fabric without nap
  Sizes 10 and 12: $2\frac{5}{8}$yd (2.4m)
  Sizes 14, 16, 18 and 20: $3\frac{1}{4}$yd (2.9m)
45 and 54in (115 and 140cm)-wide fabric with or without nap
  For all sizes: $2\frac{5}{8}$yd (2.4m)
Matching thread
Three $\frac{1}{2}$in (12mm) ball buttons
Interfacing for cuffs

Key to pattern pieces
1 Blouse front	Cut 1 on fold
2 Blouse back	Cut 1 on fold
3 Sleeve	Cut 2
4 Cuff	Cut 2
5 Facing for center front opening	Cut 1
6 Facing for sleeve opening	Cut 2

Cutting out
1 Cut out the pattern pieces following the correct line for the size you want.
2 Prepare the fabric and pin on the pattern pieces, following the layouts (shown opposite). Make sure you place the pieces with the direction lines on the correct grain of the fabric. Cut out the fabric.
3 Transfer all pattern markings.

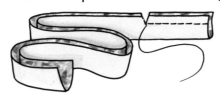

Button loop and neck binding

1 Measure the length of the neck edge. Add 1¾in (4.5cm) for loop, plus ¼in (6mm) seam allowance. Cut a 1¼in (3.2cm)-wide bias strip this length.
2 Make a tube measuring 1¾in (4.5cm) long at one end of the strip for the loop. Snip seam allowance close to end of stitching as shown.

3 Pin and baste one end of the loop to the right side of the front in position indicated on pattern.

Neck facing

  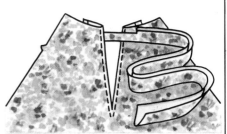

1 Finish the two long raw edges and one short edge on the neck facing by turning in ⅛in (3mm) and machine stitching. Press flat.
2 With right sides together, matching center front lines, pin, baste and stitch the neck facing to the blouse front, beginning the stitching ¼in (6mm) from the center front line at the neck edge and tapering to a point.

3 Slash between the stitching to the point and turn the facing to the wrong side.

4 Baste close to the stitched edge. Press flat.
5 Baste the facing to the neck edge. On the right side, topstitch around the opening ¼in (6mm) from the edge.

Terry Evans

Cutting layouts

36in-wide fabric with or without nap

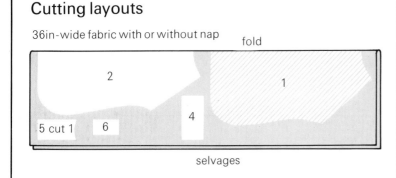

45 and 54in-wide fabric with or without nap

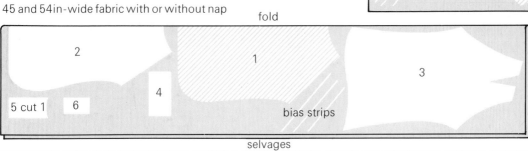

⅝in seam allowance included

John Hutchinson

Sleeve

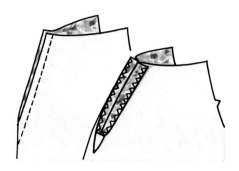

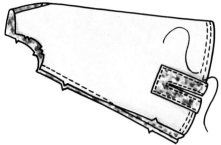

1 Apply facing to the sleeve opening in the same way as for the neck opening.

2 With right sides together, baste and stitch the shoulder dart.
3 Finish the raw edges by machine zig-zag or hand overcasting and press the seam open.

4 With right sides together, matching notches, baste and stitch the underarm sleeve seam. Finish and press seam open.
5 Run two rows of gathering stitches on lower edge of sleeve.

Applying cuffs

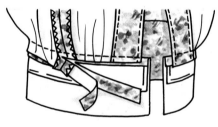

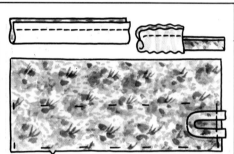

1 Baste interfacing to wrong side of cuff.

2 Make a loop of tubing for each cuff measuring $2\frac{1}{2}$in (6.5cm) long and baste to right side of cuff in position indicated on pattern.

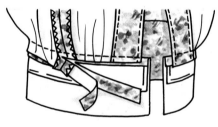

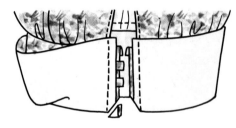

3 With right sides together, matching notches, pin, baste and stitch cuff to sleeve edge, adjusting gathers to fit cuff.

4 Grade seam allowances and press seam toward cuff.

5 With right sides together, fold cuff on fold line, baste and stitch ends as shown. Cut across corners.

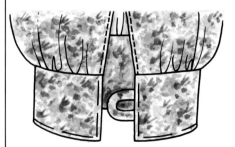

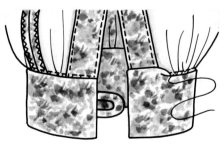

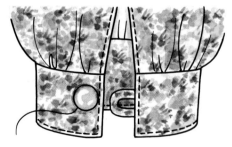

6 Turn cuff right side out and baste close to fold line.

7 Turn under seam allowance on the inside and hem by hand to the line of stitching. Press cuff flat.

8 On the right side, topstitch around outer edge of cuff $\frac{1}{4}$in (6mm) from outer edge. Press flat.
9 Sew a ball button to the cuff to correspond with the loop.

Terry Evans

*Easing
*Setting in a raglan sleeve
*Overcasting
*Narrow hem method
*Pattern for a raglan-sleeved blouse: directions for making (2)

Easing

If two pieces of a garment are to be sewed together and are slightly unequal in length, the longer piece must be eased into the shorter. Easing provides shaping to accommodate a curved area of the body, but the seam should appear smooth with no indication of a gather.

You are likely to use easing when fitting a sleeve into an armhole, or at the elbow in a long sleeve. Easing is also used on the shaped seams of a princess-line garment, or on the front section of a raglan-sleeved garment, to allow for the curve of the bust.

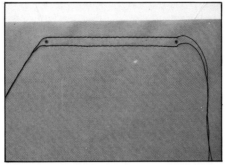

1 Wherever easing is required, the area to be eased will be marked on the pattern by notches or circles.
Adjust the sewing machine for the longest stitch and stitch between notches $\frac{1}{8}$in (3mm) from each side of the seamline on area to be eased.

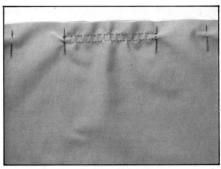

2 Pull up the thread on the wrong side until the seam edge of the longer piece is the same length as the shorter one.

3 Distribute the ease evenly and press lightly using a damp cloth to shrink out any fullness along the seamline.

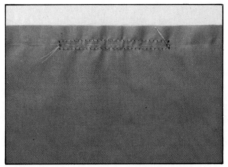

4 With right sides together, matching notches, pin the two sections together and baste.

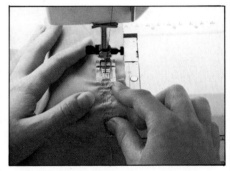

5 Whenever possible, stitch the seam with the eased seam on top.

Setting in a raglan sleeve

The deep-cut armhole of a raglan sleeve allows for ease of movement without putting strain on the garment, and the soft curve of the sleeve at the shoulder is flattering to wear.

A raglan sleeve is easier to insert than a set-in sleeve because you are working with a relatively flat seam that requires only a small amount of easing, or none at all. The shoulder of a raglan sleeve can be shaped by a shoulder dart or a seam running the length of the shoulder.

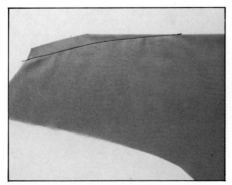

1 Baste and stitch the shoulder dart or seam on the sleeve.

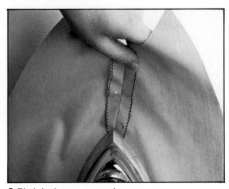

2 Finish the seam and press open.

continued

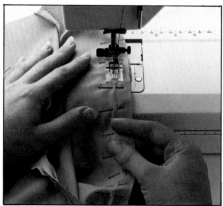

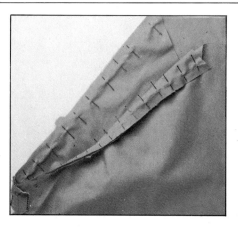

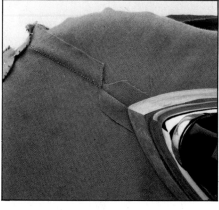

3 Baste, stitch, finish and press the sleeve underarm seam open.

4 With right sides together, keeping raw edges even and matching notches and underarm seams exactly, pin and baste the sleeve to the armhole, keeping the sleeve on top. If the garment front is eased, make sure the ease is evenly distributed.

5 Machine stitch the seam with the sleeve on top.

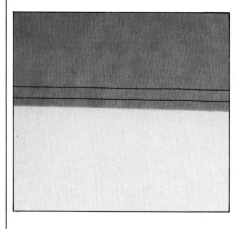

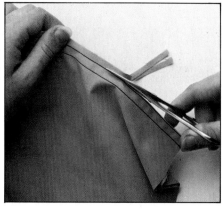

6 For fine fabrics such as voile, lawn, cotton, silk or wool challis, finish the seam allowance by working a second row of machine stitching $\frac{1}{4}$in (6mm) away from the first into the seam allowance.

7 Trim the seam allowance close to this second row of machine stitching and finish the raw edge by hand or machine overcasting. Press the seam toward the sleeve.

8 To hold the seam allowance in the correct direction and give a smooth line to the seam on the right side of the garment, work a row of topstitching through all thicknesses, $\frac{1}{8}-\frac{1}{4}$in (3mm-6mm) away from the seamline.

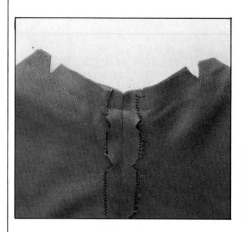

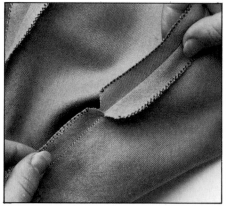

9 For a smooth seam on thicker fabrics such as dress- and suit-weight woolens and woolen/synthetic blends, stitch the sleeve into the armhole and notch the underarm seam to within 3in (8cm) on each side of the underarm seam.

10 Press this underarm area of the seam together toward the sleeve and press the rest of the seam open on each side.

11 Finish the edges of the pressed-open seam separately. Finish the edges of the underarm section together.

Overcasting

Hand overcasting is a method used to finish a seam or hem a raw edge. Although machine overcasting or zig-zag stitch can be used instead of hand overcasting in most places, there are occasions when it affects the finish of the garment. For example, on some sheer fabrics such as voile, machine zig-zagging may be too thick and heavy for the weight of fabric and may show through to the right side of the garment. Or, at an armhole edge, where a soft, comfortable finish is needed, the zig-zag may be too rough or cause a ridge on the right side of the garment when the seam is pressed.

1 If the raw edge has raveled and needs trimming, trim and overcast just a small section at a time.

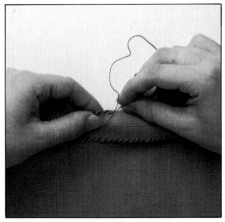

2 Start with a double backstitch and make small, diagonally-sloping, evenly-spaced stitches. Do not pull the stitches tight; let them lie on the fabric.

Narrow hem method

This method gives a neat, narrow and strong hem. It is useful for blouse and shirt hems, especially if they are to be tucked into a skirt or slacks, since it gives the least amount of bulk in the hem. It is also useful on fine or sheer fabrics, where a deeper hem would show on the right side of the garment. It is particularly good for use on full-length garments made in fine fabrics, since the row of machine stitching used to finish the raw edge gives the hem considerable strength in wear.

1 Mark the hem $\frac{1}{4}$in (6mm) below the required finished hem level.

2 With right side on top, turn under seam allowance on marked line, baste.

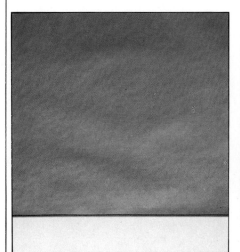

3 Stitch close to the folded edge.

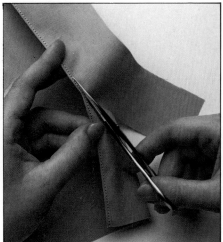

4 On the wrong side, trim away the excess fabric close to the line of stitching.

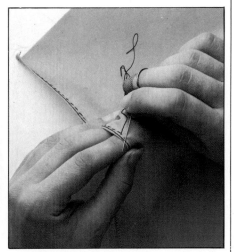

5 Turn up the hem $\frac{1}{4}$in (6mm) and hem by hand. Press hem flat on wrong side.

Paul Williams

Raglan-sleeved blouse: directions for making (2)

Side seams and sleeve

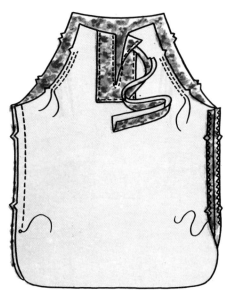

1 On the blouse front, run two rows of gathering stitches between notches for easing. With right sides together, matching notches and circles, baste and stitch the side seams to circles. Finish and press seams open.

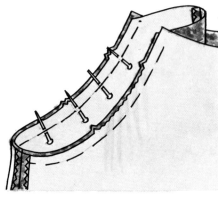

2 With right sides together, matching underarm seams and notches, pin the sleeve to the blouse, pulling up the ease evenly. Baste.

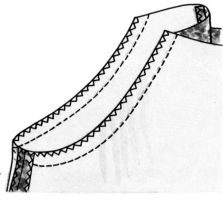

3 Stitch the seam. Finish with overcasting or zig-zag stitch, according to the type of fabric you are using. Press the seam.

Jean-Claude Volpelière

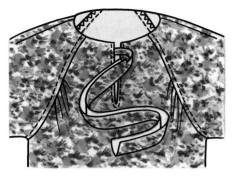

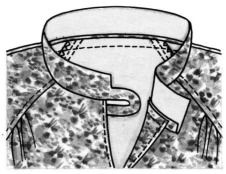

2 Stitch binding into place, taking ¼in (6mm) seam allowance. Press seam away from blouse.

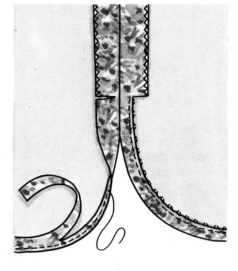

2 Turn up another ⅛in (3mm) and hand hem.

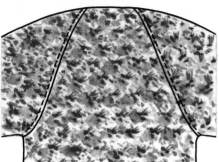

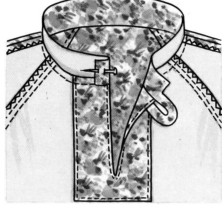

3 With wrong sides together, turn back the ¼in (6mm) seam allowance of the binding at the center front and pin.

4 If using a fine fabric, topstitch this armhole seam.

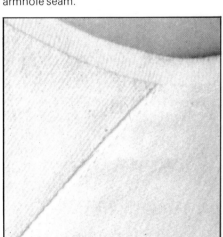

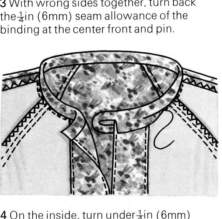

4 On the inside, turn under ¼in (6mm) seam allowance of the binding and hem the folded edge to the line of stitching. Press the bound edge flat.

Finishing

Neck binding

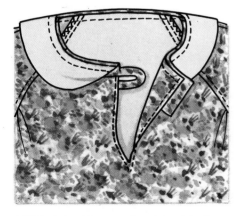

1 With right sides together, baste binding to neck edge, forming a loop at center front as shown and leaving ¼in (6mm) seam allowance extending at opposite center front neck edge.

1 Machine finish and turn up a narrow hem at the blouse lower edge. Press flat.

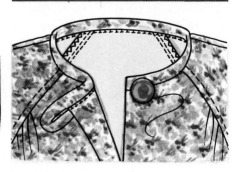

3 Sew a ball button to the center front neck edge to correspond with buttonhole loop.

67

Needlework

Step-by-step course – 1

The basics of needlepoint

Needlepoint is one of the oldest forms of needlework. It lends itself to a wide variety of designs, both modern and traditional, intricate and simple, and produces a hard-wearing surface that is suitable for many household items such as pillow covers and chair seats as well as fashion accessories such as belts and bags. Using only the basic stitch—called tent stitch—you can create your own original designs.

Canvas

The two types of canvas most often used for needlepoint are mono, a single-thread weave, and Penelope, a double-thread weave in which the two threads in each strand can be used separately to produce tiny as well as larger stitches. Both types are available in a wide variety of gauges (threads per inch). Choose a fine gauge and fine thread for a small-scale or intricate design and a larger gauge and thicker thread for a design with less detail. Be sure the canvas has even holes and smooth threads.

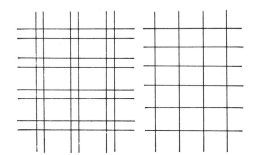

Needles

Tapestry (or needlepoint) needles have large eyes to hold thick thread, and blunt ends that will not split the canvas threads. They come in a variety of sizes. Choose a needle that does not stretch the holes of the canvas but is large enough to carry the yarn easily.

Thread

A wide range of thread is available for needlepoint. Traditionally, Persian, tapestry, crewel and rug yarn have been used, but you may also use cotton embroidery floss or silk or rayon thread if you prefer. The thread should be of good quality with long, smooth and durable fibers that will not break when it is pulled through the canvas. Be sure to use thread that is colorfast and mothproof.

Other equipment

One of the attractions of needlepoint is that it requires very little equipment. A few extra items, however, are helpful.
1 Small, sharp-pointed scissors to snip yarn and remove mistakes.
2 Masking tape to bind the raw edges of canvas during work to prevent fraying.
3 Indelible marking pen to mark the design on the canvas.
4 Acrylic or oil paint may be used to paint the design on canvas. It must be indelible. Experiment to make sure.
5 Graph paper for working out designs.

Canvas	Thread*	Needle
18–22	1 strand Persian 2 strands crewel	22–24
14–16	2 strands Persian tapestry 3 strands crewel	18–20
10–12	3 strands Persian tapestry 4 strands crewel	18–20
5–8	5–6 strands Persian	14–18
	rug yarn	darning needle

*for tent stitch

Threading the needle

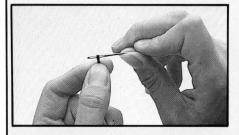

1 Loop yarn over needle and fold to make a crease. Remove needle.

2 Push fold through eye of needle. Pull short end of thread through.

Simon Butcher

Starting

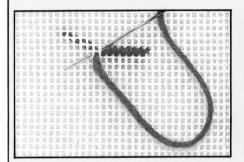

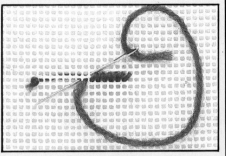

1 Insert needle from wrong side leaving a 1 in (2.5cm) tail. Cover tail with backs of first few stitches.

2 Or, knot thread. Insert needle from top a few holes from starting point. Cover thread as you work. Snip knot.

Finishing

Run needle and thread through several stitches on wrong side in one direction and then other, or at right angle to row.

Continental stitch

There are two varieties of tent stitch: the continental stitch and the basket weave stitch. They look alike on the front of the work, but are worked differently. The continental stitch is easier to do, but it tends to distort the canvas when it is used to cover large areas. It is used most often to work single lines or to fill in small areas of one color. For horizontal rows of continental stitches, work from right to left. Turn canvas after every row so that you are always working from right to left. Even-numbered rows will be stitched above the previous row and odd-numbered rows below.

Continental stitch may also be worked vertically from top to bottom with each new stitch just below the one completed. And it can be worked diagonally by placing stitches end to end from upper right to lower left.

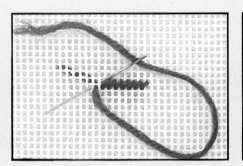

1 Bring thread to right side of canvas one hole below and one to the left of upper right-hand corner of area to be stitched. Work stitch diagonally up and to right over one canvas mesh (intersection). Pass needle down and to left behind canvas, bringing it up one hole to left of bottom of first stitch. Complete row with thread at back.

2 Turn canvas so bottom is at top and work the second row from right to left *above* the first. To start, bring needle up through hole used for the top of the second stitch below and reinsert it one hole above and to right over one mesh. Turn canvas and work third row from right to left *below* the second row.

Basket weave stitch

The basket weave stitch distorts the canvas less than the continental stitch and may be used to cover large areas such as the background in a design. In basket weave, rows of stitches run diagonally from upper left to lower right and from lower right to upper left alternately. Work begins in the upper right-hand corner of the area to be covered. The corner stitch is worked diagonally up and to the right over one canvas mesh. The needle emerges one hole to the left of the bottom of the first stitch ready for the first row.

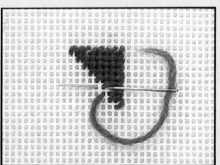

1 Upper left to lower right row: work stitches diagonally up and to right over one canvas mesh. Take needle down vertically at back bringing it to front two holes below. Complete row bringing needle up one hole below bottom of last stitch ready for next row.

2 Lower right to upper left row: work stitches diagonally up and to right over one canvas mesh. Take needle horizontally across back and bring it up two holes to left ready for next stitch. Work third row as first, beginning one hole to left of bottom of the last stitch.

Cool coasters

Design these bright needlepoint coasters yourself and make them in basic needlepoint stitches.

Our coasters are 3½in (9cm) square. You can make your any size, following this basic design.

Materials

For each coaster:
4½in (11.5cm) square of No. 16 mono canvas
1 skein of tapestry yarn in each of several colors (we used 4)
No. 20 tapestry needle
3½in (9cm) square piece of felt for backing
Masking tape, indelible marking pen
Crewel wool to match, crewel needle

To make

1 Bind the edges of the canvas square with masking tape to prevent fraying.
2 Find the center of the canvas and mark with a cross on the threads using the indelible pen.
3 Decide on a simple design. Blocks or stripes of color are easy to work; we used 8 blocks across and 8 down. Each is 7 stitches square. If you wish, mark your design on the canvas with the pen.
4 Cut a piece of tapestry yarn about 20in (51cm).
5 Thread tapestry needle and work from the center outward, using continental or basket weave stitches or both.
6 Continue working to fill every hole in a 3½in (9cm) square.
7 If the canvas becomes distorted in shape as you work, steam press it on the wrong side to ease it gently back into a square when you have finished.
8 Remove masking tape and fold unstitched edges to wrong sides so the stitched area shows on top. Press.
9 Pin and baste the felt square to the wrong side of the canvas.
10 Using crewel wool and needle, sew felt to canvas with tiny blanket stitches. Press.

Paul Williams

Needlework / COURSE 2

*Preparing the canvas
*Tracing the design
*Blocking
*Mounting a pillow cover
*Making a butterfly pillow cover

Making a needlepoint pillow cover

Pillow covers are one of the most popular and practical uses for needlepoint. They can be made in any size and shape and in colors to carry out your decorating scheme. Or they can portray your interest in flowers, animals, oriental rugs, op art or travel. Elaborate effects can be achieved with a wide variety of stitches, but simple stitches combined with color and design can produce equally effective results.

In this course we show you how to make a simple needlepoint pillow cover, from preparing the canvas to inserting the zipper. We give you a bright butterfly design to practice on. Or you may prefer to design your own cover using our instructions as a guide.

Preparing the canvas

Before buying the canvas, measure the pillow you plan to cover or buy a pillow form and measure it. The cover top should be 1in (2.5cm) smaller all around than the pillow. Work out your design on drawing paper within a border the exact size of the finished pillow cover top. Then select canvas of an appropriate gauge for the design—a fine mesh for a delicate or detailed look and a larger gauge for a bolder appearance—and buy a piece at least 6in (15cm) longer and wider than your design. If the canvas is creased, press it with a dry iron before beginning work.

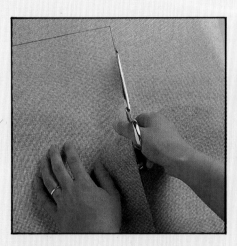

1 Cut canvas, if necessary, so that it is 2-3in (5-7.5cm) larger all around than the finished embroidery will be. Make a note of the size of the canvas.

2 Fold a strip of masking tape over each edge of the canvas to keep threads from catching while you are working and to prevent raveling.

3 Fold the canvas across its width and then its length to find the center mesh (intersection of threads).

4 Mark the center mesh with a penciled cross. Extend the 4 arms of the cross out to the centers of the 4 edges of the canvas. Mark these lines on the back also if they do not show through.

5 Measure out from the center to find the sides of the embroidery area (the last mesh to be covered in the design) and mark along each side with a pencil.

Tracing the design

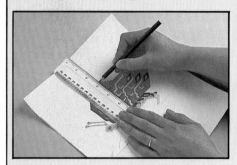  

1 Ink in the lines on your design and the border around it to make them stand out. Find the center of the design and mark it with a penciled cross. Extend the arms of the cross out to the edges with pencil. Place your design under the canvas and then match the center lines and borders.

2 Copy the design onto the canvas in pencil or indelible pen, starting with major shapes and gradually filling in the detail. If your canvas is so fine that you cannot see the design through it, transfer the design to the canvas with dressmaker's tracing (carbon) paper.

3 If you wish, you may paint your canvas in the colors you intend to use in your needlepoint. This helps hide the canvas if the thread does not completely cover it. Otherwise, use the colors on the design as a guide.

Blocking finished needlepoint

 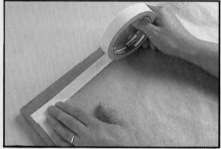 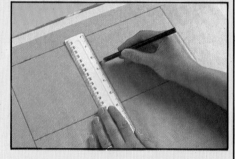

1 If your canvas has become soiled as you worked, you may wipe it lightly with a cloth dampened with cleaning fluid to restore brightness.

2 Cover a large board, piece of plywood or old table top with strong brown paper and tape the paper to the board with masking tape.

3 On the paper draw an outline the size of your canvas before you began working on it. Use a T square or triangle to make sure the corners are square. Draw a horizontal and a vertical line through the center of the shape.

 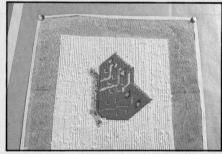 

4 Spray your needlepoint with water using a plant sprayer or wet it with a sponge. It should be thoroughly wet but not soaked or dripping.

5 Place the needlepoint face down on the paper and tack the corners of the canvas to the corners drawn on the paper, stretching to fit from opposite sides as necessary. Use thumb tacks or push pins and hammer them in if necessary to make sure they hold.

6 Tack the center of each side of the canvas to the center of each side of the shape on the paper matching the lines on both. Then, moving around the canvas, place a tack in the middle of each open space. Continue until tacks are about $\frac{1}{2}$ in (1.3cm) apart. Leave the canvas for 24 to 48 hours or until it is completely dry before removing tacks.

Frederick Mancini

Mounting a pillow cover

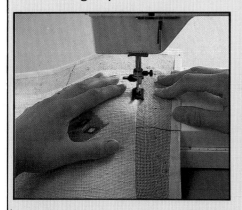

1 Machine stitch around the needlepointed area of the canvas just outside the last row of stitches to prevent raveling.

2 Cut off taped edges of canvas. Cut out a piece of backing material the same size as the trimmed canvas.

3 With right sides together, stitch the backing to the needlepointed top of the pillow cover leaving one side open. The machine stitches should go through the last row of needlepoint stitches so that no unworked canvas shows along the seam on the right side.

4 Trim the seams to ½in (1.3cm) and cut off corners diagonally close to the stitching to eliminate bulk.

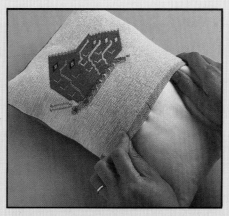

5 Turn pillow cover right side out and insert pillow through open side.

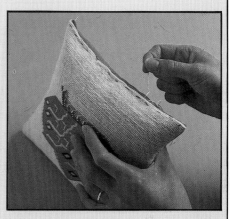

6 Whipstitch opening to complete cover.

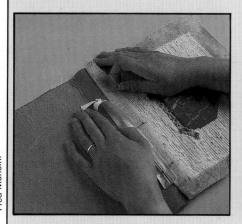

7 If you wish to insert a zipper, put it in before stitching the pillow back to the top. Right sides together, baste top to back along one side. Mark placement of zipper in the center of this side with pins at each end and stitch from these pins to the corners. Press seam open.

8 Open out cover and lay face down. Place zipper face down with teeth along seam. Baste tape on one side of zipper to seam allowance of front and back. Stitch along top, side and bottom of zipper.

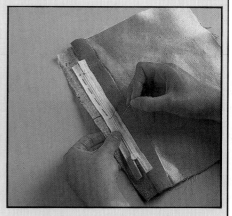

9 Fold top of cover under back leaving seam allowance of top extended under unstitched zipper tape. Baste and stitch free side of zipper to top seam allowance. Pin, baste and stitch remaining 3 sides of cover. Turn right side out and stuff.

John Hutchinson

Accent on color

Brighten your room with a butterfly pillow. Choose your own colors and add flowers if you wish.

Note: For our pillow cover, we used a small 9in (23cm) square pillow form and No. 18 canvas to produce a delicate effect. You may prefer to work the design on a No. 10 or 12 canvas for a bolder look. If so, use the main lines of the design and simplify or eliminate the detail as necessary. If you wish to make a larger pillow cover, add flowers (see suggested design shown above) in corners or around edges to extend the design. Or have the butterfly design enlarged by a photocopying service before transferring it to the canvas. In this case, you can use a larger gauge canvas without giving up any of the detail.

Materials
(These materials are for the pillow shown. For an extended design or a larger pillow cover, you will need a larger canvas, more embroidery wool, more backing material, and a larger zipper if used.)

No. 18 canvas, 15in (38cm)-square
*   piece*
Masking tape
Pencil and ruler
Dressmaker's tracing (carbon) paper
Indelible marking pen (optional)
Waterproof acrylic paints or
*   waterproof felt-tip pens (optional)*

Tapestry wool: 1 15-yd (13.7m) skein
*   each of two shades of yellow, two*
*   oranges, two greens and two blues;*
*   5 skeins of white*
No. 20 tapestry needle
Sharp-pointed embroidery scissors
Flat wooden surface for blocking
Heavy brown paper
T-square or right triangle
Rustproof thumb tacks or push pins
*   and a hammer*
Plant sprayer or sponge
½yd (.4m) synthetic silk curtain fabric
*   for pillow back*
6in (15cm) zipper (optional)
Sewing thread to match pillow back

To make
1 Prepare canvas (see page 71).
2 Transfer design to canvas (see page 72) and color if you wish. Do not worry if the lines of the drawing do not correspond exactly with the meshes of the canvas.
3 Cut embroidery thread into pieces about 18in (46cm) long. You may want to use several needles threaded with different colors rather than re-thread each time you change color.
4 Start by outlining the wings and body of the butterfly in continental stitch worked in horizontal, vertical and diagonal rows as necessary. Be sure all the stitches slant in the same direction. Where the line of the design crosses a mesh, you will have to decide which color to use. Remember that curved and diagonal lines in the design must be stepped on the canvas. Finish each end of each thread as you go along (see page 69). Dark threads should be woven behind dark stitches so they will not show through on the front. Be sure to carry threads loosely so they will not distort the canvas. Roll the canvas to make it easier to hold as you work.
5 Work the small blocks of color within wings and body in continental stitch.
6 Using continental stitch, fill remaining areas of wings in horizontal rows.
7 Starting at the upper right-hand corner of the pillow cover, work the background in basket weave stitch. Remember to alternate the direction of each row to avoid ridges on the completed work.
8 If you make a mistake, remove the needle from the thread and use the eye to pull it out. Snip the thread leaving a tail to weave in. To remove several stitches, cut them out carefully with your embroidery scissors.
9 If thread becomes twisted, hold the canvas up letting the needle dangle on the end of the thread. It will untwist.
10 Hold completed canvas to the light to check that every mesh has been covered with a stitch.
11 Block the canvas (see page 72).
12 Mount the canvas as a pillow cover following directions on page 73.
13 Make tassels by winding yarn 30-40 times around a piece of cardboard the length of tassel. Run piece of yarn under threads at one end and tie. Cut threads at opposite end. Wind wool around tassel 1-2in (2.5-5cm) below tied end. Tie. Bury ends in tassel.

Needlework / COURSE 3

Quilting

Quilting was used centuries ago to produce warm clothing and bedding by sewing several layers of fabric together. The stitching produced a raised effect that was decorative as well as practical. Today quilting is still used to produce warm fabrics. But the raised effect of the stitching also makes the quilted fabric popular for many household items that need not be warm such as tablecloths, toaster covers, laundry bags, placemats and even rugs. You can make many of these items yourself at home by hand or machine. In this course we help you learn how.

Materials

To get the best results in quilting, use a soft, closely woven fabric for the top and bottom layers and one or more layers of cotton or polyester batting for the filling. Polyester filling is as soft and fluffy as cotton and has the advantage of being machine washable. The thicker the filling, the softer and warmer the fabric will be, but the stitching will show up more clearly with a thinner filling.

The quilting may be done with quilting thread for a slightly glossy effect or with regular sewing thread in the same material as the top layer of fabric. The thread may be in a color that complements the top layer of fabric or contrasts with it. In machine quilting, you may also use different color threads on the top and on the bobbin—one to complement or contrast with the top fabric and the other with the bottom.

Use crewel needles or short, sharp betweens for hand quilting. For machine stitching choose a sharp needle in a medium size.

If you plan to quilt a large item such as a bedspread by hand, your work will be easier with a quilting frame. There are a number of styles available. Choose one that holds all the layers of the fabric taut and the corners square. For smaller projects, a large hoop is helpful. You may quilt by hand without a frame or hoop, but if you do, be sure to baste all layers together securely with backstitches in many horizontal, vertical and diagonal rows across the fabric. For machine quilting, no frame or hoop is necessary.

Starting and ending

In hand quilting, tie a small knot in the end of your thread. Insert the needle from the bottom at your starting point and gently pull the knot through the lower layer of the fabric. It will embed itself in the batting. Then proceed with a stitch in the upper layer. To end a thread, bring the needle to the top layer and take two tiny stitches where the next stitch will cover them. Then take a long stitch under the top layer and part of the batting and bring the needle up about 1in (2.5 cm) away. Cut the thread near the surface. The end will slip through the top layer and get lost in the batting.

Transferring the design

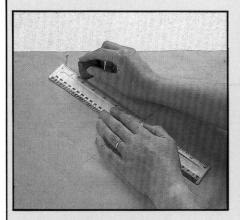

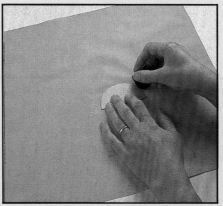

1 Cut top layer 1–2in (2.5–5cm) larger all around than finished size. Transfer design to top layer only. For simple repeat designs, work out spacing of lines within area to be quilted on graph paper. The quilting lines should be 2–3in (5–7.5cm) apart. If the lines are all straight and the design is simple, draw the design on the right side of the top layer with a ruler and tailor's chalk.

2 For curved lines or more complex straight line patterns, work out the spacing on graph paper and then make one or more templates out of cardboard. Place the template on the fabric as many times as required and trace around with chalk or pencil.

3 For non-repeat designs, work out the motif on drawing paper, enlarge it to the required size, and transfer it to the fabric with dressmaker's carbon paper.

Assembling the layers

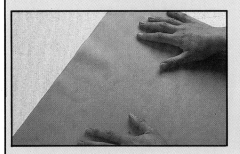 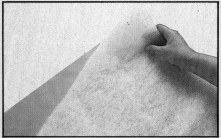 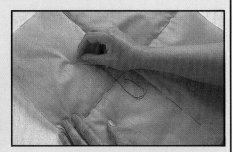

1 Cut the batting and the bottom layer the same size as the top layer. Lay the bottom fabric wrong side up on a flat surface.

2 Center the batting, one layer at a time if more than one layer is used, on top of the backing and carefully smooth it out from the center to the edges.

3 Center the top layer on the batting right side up. Baste the 3 layers together starting at the center and working out to the center of each side and then to each corner. Baste around the outer edges. The fabric is now ready for the frame or for machine quilting.

Quilting

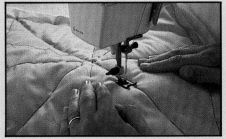 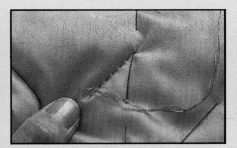 

1 By machine. Use regular presser foot, a long, straight stitch, and slightly heavier pressure than you would use for a medium-weight fabric. Begin at the center and stitch part way out in one direction, then another, following the lines marked on the fabric. Continue working out toward all the edges in stages. When the quilting is finished, trim the edges to even them.

2 For hand quilting thick fabrics. Working from the center out, place one hand under the fabric and the other on top. Insert the needle from the bottom in a stabbing motion and pull it through the top. Push needle down from the top and pull it through the bottom. Each stitch on the top and bottom should be about $\frac{1}{8}$in (3mm) long. Thread several needles and use one to work about 6in (15cm) out from the center in one direction. Then switch needle and work out in another direction.

3 For hand quilting thinner fabrics. Hold the fabric between thumb and fingers of one hand, take several stitches and pull the thread through with the other. The stitches should be about $\frac{1}{8}$in (3mm) long on both the top and bottom. Work out from the center in all directions as in Step 2.

Some quilting patterns

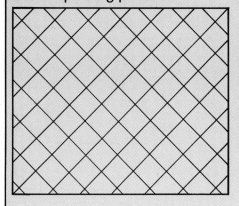 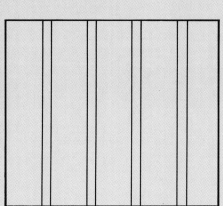 

Simon Butcher

Soft setting

Quick and easy quilting makes these pretty, practical placemats. Choose washable fabrics to coordinate with your dining room or kitchen. You can vary the quilting pattern from mat to mat for practice and a more individual look.

Materials
For one mat:
*2 pieces of closely woven fabric
14 x 17in (36 x 43cm) each
matching or contrasting thread
1 layer of polyester batting 14 x 17in
(36 x 43cm)
4 pieces of 2in (5cm)-wide bias
strips of contrasting fabric: 2
strips 13in (35cm) long; 2 strips
17in (43cm) long
matching thread
long ruler and pencil or chalk*

To make
1 Iron all fabrics.

2 Using a long ruler and tailor's chalk, or a light pencil, mark a point 1½in (4cm) in from each corner, 1in (2.5cm) from each side.
3 Draw a line from the point in the upper left-hand corner to the point in the lower right-hand corner.
4 On each side of this line and parallel to it, draw more lines 2in (5cm) apart.
5 Draw a line from the point in the upper right-hand corner to the lower left-hand corner and draw lines parallel to it as in step 4.
6 Assemble the layers and baste them together (see page 77).
7 Prepare machine (see page 77).

Holding fabric taut and flat with both hands on each side of the presser foot, stitch from center along marked lines to the four corners making a large X. Then stitch the lines on each side of the two arms of the X. Continue working out toward the corners. Be especially careful where lines of stitching cross that material does not pleat.
8 Remove basting.
9 Trim mat evenly all around to finished size.
10 Right sides together and edges matching, pin and baste the 13in (33cm) strips to the short edges of the top layer of the mat. Stitch ½in (1.3cm) from edge. Remove basting.
11 Fold the strip over the raw edge. Turn under ½in (1.3cm) and pin, baste and hand stitch to bottom of mat.
12 Repeat with the 17in (43cm) strips on the long edges of the mat folding in the ends to make square corners.

Shoestring

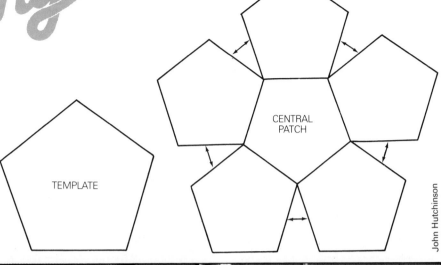

TEMPLATE

CENTRAL PATCH

John Hutchinson

Lavender blue

These pretty patchwork balls hold lavender to bring a sweet fragrance to your closet.

Materials for each
Tracing paper
Cardboard
Scraps of fabric in four different but coordinating prints
Iron-on interfacing
5in (12cm) piece of cord
12in (30cm) of narrow ribbon
Lavender, about ½oz (15g)
Suitable filling
Matching thread

1 Trace the pattern for the template. Transfer it to cardboard by pressing down firmly with a ballpoint pen. Cut out carefully.
2 Using template, mark 12 patches on wrong (non-shiny) side of interfacing. Cut out 12 patches.
3 Pin three interfacing patches on the wrong side of each piece of fabric, leaving at least ¼in (5mm) all around each patch.
4 Iron interfacing patches in place.
5 Cut out each interfaced fabric patch, adding a ¼in (5mm) border outside interfacing.
6 On each patch, fold the border over the interfaced center, each side in turn; pin and baste. Make sure the folded edges are accurate and the corners sharp.
7 Join the patches as follows: place two patches together exactly, right sides facing. Overcast along one edge with tiny stitches. Sew five patches together around a central patch for each half, as shown, alternating the fabrics.
8 Join the adjacent sides of the five outer patches of each half, then join the two halves together in the same way, leaving two sides unstitched. Remove basting stitches. Turn ball right side out.
9 Fill ball with a mixture of filling and lavender.
10 Neatly overcast the last two seams, inserting the folded cord at one corner for hanging the ball.
11 Tie ribbon in a bow around base of cord. Snip ribbon ends into V shapes for a neat finish.

Gary Warren

Funny bunnies

More experienced crochet addicts can work the front view of the rabbit for the front bib and the back view of the rabbit for the back of these playsuits and make socks to match.

Peter Pugh-Cook

Sizes

Playsuits To fit 18[20]in (46[51]cm) chest.
Length from top of bib to crotch, 13½[14½]in (34[37]cm).
Socks Foot seam, 3½[4]in (9[10]cm). Bottom of heel to top of sock, 7[7½]in (18[19]cm).
Note Directions for larger size are in brackets []; where there is only one set of figures it applies to both sizes.

Materials

5[6]oz (120[140]g) of a sport yarn in main color A
1oz (20g) in each of 2 contrasting colors (B and C)
No. 0 steel and sizes C and E (2.00, 3.00 and 3.50mm) crochet hooks
2 buttons

Gauge

21 hdc and 14 rows to 4in (10cm) on size E (3.50mm) hook.

Playsuits

Front

Using size E (3.50mm) hook and A, make 24[28]ch for top of bib.
Base row 1 hdc into 3rd ch from hook, 1 hdc into each ch to end. Turn. 23[27] sts.
Patt row 2ch to count as first hdc, 1 hdc into each hdc to end, 1 hdc into top of turning ch. Turn.
Rep the patt row 6 times more.
Inc row 2ch, 1 hdc into first hdc, 2 hdc into next hdc, 1 hdc into each hdc to within last 2 hdc, 2 hdc into next hdc, 2 hdc into last hdc. Turn. (4 hdc increased in row.) 27[31] hdc. Patt 1 row. Rep the last 2 rows once more. 31[35] hdc. Fasten off.

Waistline

Next row Make 7 ch, work 1 hdc into each hdc across lower edge of bib section, make 8 ch. Turn.
Next row 1 hdc into 3rd ch from hook, 1 hdc into each of next 5 ch, 1 hdc into each of the 31[35] hdc on bib, then 1 hdc into each of rem 7 ch. 45[49] sts.
Cont in patt until work measures 13[14½]in (34[37]cm) from top of bib.
***Divide for legs
1st leg Work across first 23[25] hdc, turn.
Next row Make 5 ch, work 1 hdc into 3rd ch from hook, 1 hdc into each of the next 2 ch, 1 hdc into each of next 23[25] hdc. Turn. 27[29] hdc.
****Work 2 rows without shaping.
Inc row 2ch, 1 hdc into first hdc, 1 hdc into each hdc, 2 hdc into turning ch. Turn. 29[31] hdc. Patt 6 rows. Work inc row again, then cont without shaping until leg measures 5[5½]in (12.5[13.5]cm). Fasten off.
2nd leg Make 4 ch, then work 1 hdc into the 23rd [25th] hdc of first leg (i.e. into the same hdc as last st on first row of first leg), now work 1 hdc into each hdc to end. Turn. 23[25] hdc.

Next row Patt to last 4 ch, then work 1 hdc into each of the 4 ch. Turn. 27[29] sts. Complete to match first leg from ** to end.

Back

Work as for front to within 2 rows of division for legs.
Next row Patt to last 6 sts, 1 sc into next st, turn.
Next row 1 ch, skip sc, 1 sc into first hdc, 1 hdc into each hdc to within last 6 sts, 1 sc into next st, turn.
Rep last row 4 times more.
Next row Work to end.
Next row Work to end.
Now complete as for front from *** to end.

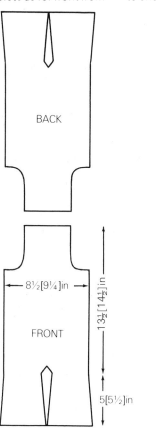

BACK

FRONT

8½[9¼]in

13½[14½]in

5[5½]in

To finish

Join side seams and inside leg seams to within 6 rows of lower edge of leg. Turn to RS and sew remainder of seam. Using size C (3.00mm) hook and A, work 1 sc into each st around lower edge of leg, do not turn but work a row of crab st (sc worked from left to right), sl st into first st. Fasten off. Finish lower edge of other leg to match.

Left strap

Using size C (3.00mm) hook and A, make 18[20] ch, then with RS facing work 1 sc into the first row end of the left side of back bib, working along armhole edge work (2 sc into next row end, 1 sc into next row end) 9 times, 1 sc into each of 6 foundation ch at underarm, now work (1 sc into next row end, 2 sc into next row end) 9 times, 1 sc into last row end at top of bib, make 19[21] ch, turn.

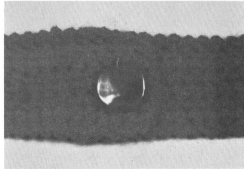

John Hutchinson

Next row 1 sc into 2nd ch from hook, 1 sc into each ch, 1 sc into each sc around armhole, then 1 sc into each of the 18[20] ch.
Buttonhole row 1 ch; 1 sc into each sc to within last 4 sc, 2 ch, skip next 2 sc, 1 sc into each of last 2 sc. Turn.
Next row 1 ch, 1 sc into each of first 2 sc, 2 sc into ch sp, then work 1 sc into each sc to end. Turn.
Next row 1 ch, 1 sc into each sc to end. Turn.
Rep last row once more. Fasten off.
Using No. 0 (2.00mm) steel hook and A, work a row of crab st. Fasten off.

Right strap
Work as for left strap but start working into the row ends of front bib first and make buttonhole at beg of row thus:
1 ch, 1 sc into each of first 2 sc, 2 ch, skip next 2 sc, 1 sc into each sc to end. Turn.
Neck edging (back and front alike)
Using size C (3.00mm) hook, A and with RS facing work 1 sc into each foundation ch on strap, 1 sc into each st across bib, then 1 sc into each foundation ch on other strap. Do not turn. Change to No. 0 (2.00mm) steel hook and work a row of crab st. Fasten off. Sew buttons on back straps to correspond with buttonholes. Press very lightly according to the directions on yarn wrapper.

Rabbit motif
Body
Using size C (3.00mm) hook and B, make 3 ch, sl st into first ch to form a circle.
1st round Work 8 sc into circle.
2nd round 2 sc into each sc all around.
3rd and every foll alternate round 1 sc into each sc all around.
4th round (1 sc into next sc, 2 sc into next sc) 8 times. 24 sc.
6th round (2 sc into next sc, 1 sc into each of next 2 sc) 8 times, 32 sc.
8th round (1 sc into each of next 3 sc, 2 sc into next sc) 8 times, 40 sc.
10th round (2 sc into next sc, 1 sc into each of next 4 sc) 8 times, 48 sc.
11th round 1 sc into each sc all around.
12th round Working from left to right work a row of crab st, sl st into first st. Fasten off.

Head
Work as for body up to and including the 7th round, then work the crab st edging. Fasten off.

Ears (make 2)
Using size C (3.00mm) hook and C, make 6 ch.
Base row 1 sc into 2nd ch from hook, 1 sc into each of next 3 ch, 3 sc into last ch, then working along other side of ch work 1 sc into each of next 4 ch. Turn.
Next row 1 ch, 1 sc into each sc to center sc of 3 sc of previous row, 3 sc into this sc, then work 1 sc into each sc to end. Turn. Cut off B, join on A.

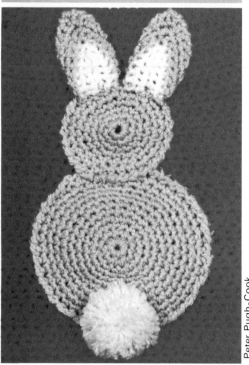

Rep last row twice more, then work a row of crab st.
Fasten off.
On flat edge of ear fold outer edges to center and sew in place.

To finish
For front view of rabbit, sew ears to back of head. Sew motif to bib, with head overlapping body slightly. Embroider eyes and whiskers on head.
For back view of rabbit, sew ears to front of head. Sew motif to bib, with body overlapping head slightly. Using C, make a small pompom for the tail and sew it to the body at the bottom of the circle.

Socks
Using size C (3.00mm) hook and A, make 28 ch, taking care not to twist the ch, sl st into first ch to form a circle.
1st round 2 ch, 1 hdc into each ch to end, sl st into top of first 2 ch. Turn.
2nd round 2 ch, skip first hdc, 1 hdc into each hdc to end, sl st into top of first 2 ch. Turn.
Repeating round 2, work 1 round B, 1 round A, 1 round C and 1 round A. Now working in A only, work 15[17] more rounds. Fasten off.
Shape instep
Continuing in A only, skip first 9 sts, rejoin yarn to next st, work 1 hdc into this st, then 1 hdc into each of the next 9 sts, turn.
Work 4[6] rows.
Dec row 2 ch, skip first hdc, (yo, insert hook into next st, yo and draw a loop through) twice, yo and draw through all loops on hook (1 hdc decreased), 1 hdc into each hdc to within last 3 sts, dec 1 hdc, 1 hdc into last st. Turn.
Rep last row once more.
Next row 2 ch, (dec 1 hdc) twice, 1 hdc into last st. (4 sts). Fasten off.
Rejoin yarn to fasten off place at heel, 2 ch, then work 1 hdc into each of next 8 sts, working up side of foot, work (2 hdc into next row end, 1 hdc into next row end) then work 1 hdc into each of the 4 sts at top, then work (1 hdc into next row end, 2 hdc into next row end) down other side of foot, then work 1 hdc into each of the rem 9 hdc, sl st into top of first 2 ch. Turn. 46[52] sts.
Shape toe
Next row 2 ch, skip next hdc, 1 hdc into each of next 20[23] hdc, (dec 1 hdc) twice, 1 hdc into each of rem 21[24] sts, sl st into top of first 2 ch. Turn.
Next row 2 ch, skip 1 hdc, 1 hdc into each of next 19[22] sts, (dec 1 hdc) twice, 1 hdc into each of rem 20[23] hdc, sl st into top of 2 ch. Turn.
Next row 2 ch, skip next hdc, 1 hdc into each of next 18[21] sts, (dec 1 hdc) twice, 1 hdc into each of rem 19[22] sts, sl st into top of 2 ch. Fasten off.
Join foot seam. Press very lightly according to directions on yarn wrapper.

Peter Pugh-Cook

Overdress, country style

Wear this smock over a dress for a pretty, country-style look. Blocks of rose doubles form motifs around the lower edge to give a delicate open-work effect.

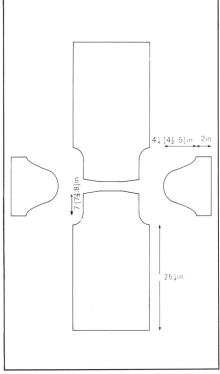

Sizes
To fit 32½ [34:36]in (83[87:92]cm) bust.
Length, 32¼ [33:33¼]in (82[84:86]cm).
Sleeve seam, 2in (5cm).
The figures in brackets [], refer to the 2nd and 3rd sizes respectively.

Gauge
24 sts and 12 rows to 4in (10cm) in dc worked on size C (3mm) hook.

Materials
*14[15:16]oz (340[360:380]g) of
    a crepe yarn
Size B (2.5mm) and C (3mm)
    crochet hooks
4 buttons*

Back
Using size C (3mm) hook chain 201 [213:225].
1st row Into 4th ch from hook work 1 dc, 1 dc into each ch to end; turn work after each row throughout. 199 [211:223] sts.
2nd row 5 ch to count as first dc and 2 ch sp, skip edge st and next 2 dc, *1 dc into next dec, 2 ch, skip 2 dc, rep from * to end, 1 dc into 3rd of 3 ch. 66[70:74] sps.
3rd row 5 ch, *1 dc into next dc, 2 ch, rep from * to end, 1 dc into 3rd of 5 ch. Rep the 3rd row until work measures 2⅜in (6cm) from beg, work in rose patt as foll:
1st row (RS) Work 2[3:4] spa, patt across next 28 sts as first row of chart, work 6[8:10] sps, patt across next 28 sts as first row of chart, work 2[3:4] sps.
2nd row Work 2[3:4] sps, patt across next 28 sts as 2nd row of chart, work 6[8:10] sps, patt across next 28 sts as 2nd row of chart, work 2[3:4] sps.
Continue in this way until the 30 rows of

chart have been completed, then continue throughout in sps as given in 3rd row, until work measures 24¾in (63cm) from beg, ending with a WS row.

Next row ch 3, *1 dc into next dc, 1 dc into sp, 1 dc into next dc, skip next sp, rep from * 31 [33:35] times more, 1 dc into next dc, 1 dc into 3rd of 5 ch. 99 [105:111] dc. Work one row in dc.

Shape armholes

1st row Sl st over first 3 sts and into 4th st, 3 ch, keeping last loop of each on hook work 1 dc into each of next 3 dc, yo and draw through all 4 loops on hook— called 3 dc tog —, work in dc to last 7 sts, 3 dc tog, 1 dc into next dc, turn. 89 [95:101] sts.

2nd row ch 3, 3 dc tog, work in dc to last 4 sts, 3 dc tog, 1 dc into 3rd of 3 ch.

3rd row 3 ch, 2 dc tog, work in dc to last 3 sts, 2 dc tog, 1 dc into 3rd of 3 ch.
Continue without shaping until armholes measure 7[8:8¾]in (18[20:22]cm) from beg, ending with a WS row.

Shape shoulders

Next row Sl st over next 5 sts, 1 sc into each of next 5 sts, 1 hdc into each of next 5 sts and 1 dc into each of next 4[5:6] sts. Cut off yarn, skip next 35 [37:39] sts, rejoin yarn to next st, 1 dc into each of next 3 [4:5] sts, 1 hdc into each of next 5 sts, 1 sc into each of next 5 sts, sl st into next 5 sts. Fasten off.

Front

Work as given for back to armhole. Shape armholes and divide for front opening.

1st row Sl st over first 3 sts and into 4th st, 3 ch, 3 dc tog, 1 dc into each of next 40 [43:46] dc, turn and continue on these sts for left front.

2nd row Patt to last 4 sts, 3 dc tog, 1 dc into 3rd of 3 ch.

3rd row 3 ch, 2 dc tog, patt to end.
Continue dec at armhole edge on next 5 [6:7] rows. 34 [36:38] sts.

Shape neck

1st row Patt to last 9 [10:11] sts, 3 dc tog, 1 dc into next dc, turn.

2nd row 3 ch, 3 dc tog, patt to end.

3rd row Patt to last 4 sts, 3 dc tog, 1 dc into 3rd of 3 ch.
Rep 2nd and 3rd rows once more, then continue without shaping on rem 19 [20:21] sts until armhole measures same as back to shoulder, ending at armhole edge.

Shape shoulder

Next row Sl st over next 5 sts, 1 sc into each of next 5 sts, 1 hdc into each of next 5 sts, 1 dc into each of next 4[5:6] dc. Fasten off. Return to where work was left, skip next 5 dc, rejoin yarn to next dc, 3 ch, patt to last 7 sts, 3 dc tog, 1 dc into next dc, turn. Complete to match left front, reversing all shaping

Sleeves

Using size C (3mm) hook chain 102 [108:114]; work first 3 rows as back. 33[35:37] sps. Rep 3rd row 3 times more.

Technique tip

How to work filet crochet from a chart

Filet crochet is the name given to the method of working doubles and chains to make a squared lace mesh.

A double is worked into the foundation chain followed by two chains. By skipping the next two chains on the foundation row and working the next double into the following chain you form a space in the work. Spaces are made in this way across the chain.

On the following row one double is worked into each double, and two chains over each space. By filling some of the spaces with blocks of two doubles a variety of patterns can be formed on the basic filet mesh.

Shape top

Next row Ch 3, 1 dc into next dc, *2 ch, 1 dc into next dc, rep from * ending with 2 ch, 1 dc into 3rd of 5 ch, turn.

Next row Ch 3, 1 dc into next dc, *2 ch, 1 dc into next dc, rep from * to last 2 dc, 2 ch, 1 dc into each of next 2 dc, turn. Rep last row to 5 sps. Fasten off.

To finish

Press with a cool iron and a dry cloth. Join shoulder seams. **Neck border** With RS facing and using size B (2.5mm) hook, work in sc around neck edge, turn and work 1 row dc. Fasten off. **Left front border** Work in sc along front edge, turn and work 3 rows dc. Fasten off. Mark 4 button positions on border, first ⅜in (1cm) from neck edge and the others 1¼in (3cm) below. **Right front border** Work as other border, but make buttonholes on 2nd row of dc by working 1 ch and skipping 1 dc and on 3rd row work 1 dc into 1 ch at each buttonhole; complete edging as foll: 1 ch, *skip next dc, (1 sc, 3 ch and

The pattern is usually drawn on graph paper, with each square on the paper representing a space or a block, and each horizontal row of squares representing one row of crochet.

Begin working the first row from the bottom right-hand corner of the graph. This will represent the first right-side row. Work in pattern across the row from right to left.

On the second row, which will be on the wrong side of the fabric, work from left to right following the graph exactly, so that each empty square will be a space and each square with an X in it will be a block of two doubles.

Remember that you will also work one double at each side of this space so that the block will consist of four doubles altogether, but when you work two blocks side by side there will be a total of only seven doubles.

Continue to work from the graph, working the uneven rows from right to left on the right side of the work and the even numbered rows from left to right on the wrong side of the work.

1 sc) into next dc, skip next sc, 1 sc into next sc, rep from * up right front, around neck and down left front. Fasten off. Set in sleeves. Join side and sleeve seams. Overlap borders at base of opening. Work edging around lower edge and sleeves. Sew on buttons.

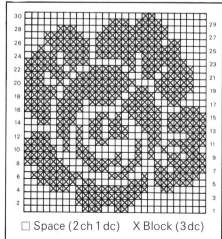

☐ Space (2 ch 1 dc)   X Block (3 dc)

Hang up your washing !

Take it on vacation or hang it on your door—this pretty, packable laundry bag is a great substitute for a bulky hamper or basket.

Materials
$\frac{7}{8}$yd (.7m) of 36in (90cm)-wide crisp cotton or linen
Matching sewing thread
A wooden coat hanger

1 Cut out the three pieces as shown on the diagram.

2 Make a double hem along the bottom edge of front A—turn under $\frac{1}{4}$in (5mm), then a further $\frac{3}{8}$in (1cm). Topstitch.

3 Turn under a double hem in the same way along the top edge of front B.

4 Lap the top edge of front B over the bottom of front A by $\frac{3}{8}$in (1cm) and pin in place at the sides.

5 With right sides together, pin the back to the fronts. Machine stitch all around $\frac{1}{4}$in (5mm) from the edge, leaving a $\frac{1}{4}$in

(5mm) opening in the center of the top edge to slip the hanger through.

6 Turn the bag right side out and press. Slip the hanger into place.

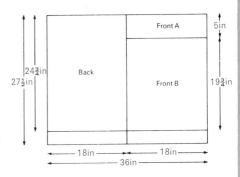

EXTRA SPECIAL CROCHET

If you think crochet is just for doilies, think again! This rugged pullover, with its ingenious basket-weave texture, is sure to please the man in your life. The woven effect comes from working double crochets around each other.

Man-appeal sweater

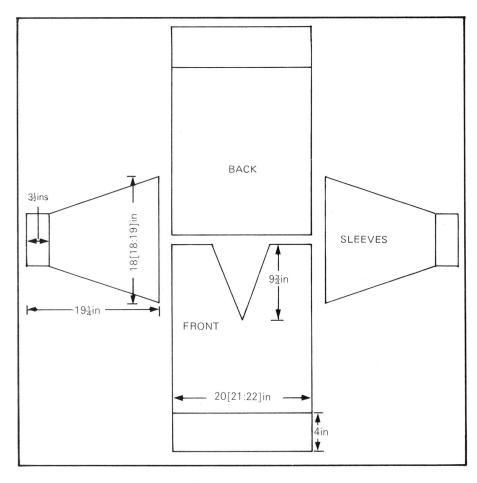

Sizes

To fit 38[40:42]in (97[102:107]cm).
Length, 27½[27½:28]in (70[70:71]cm).
Sleeve seam, 19¼in (49cm).

Materials

*43[43:45]oz (1200[1200:1250]g) of
bulky knitting yarn
Size K (7.00mm) crochet hook
No. 7 (5mm) knitting needles*

Gauge

11 sts to 4in worked on size K (7.00mm)
crochet hook.

Front

Using size K (7.00mm) hook make
56[60:64] ch.
Base row 1 dc into 3rd ch from hook,
1 dc into each ch to end. Turn. 54[58:62]
sts not counting turning ch.
Begin patt.
1st row RS, 2 ch, work around each of
next 4[1:3] dc by working yo, insert hook
from front to back between next 2 dc,
around dc at left and through work from
back to front; draw yarn through and
complete dc in usual way—called
1 double around front (dc around Ft)—,
work around each of next 5 dc by working
yo, insert hook from back to front
between next 2 dc, around dc at left
and through work from front to back;
draw yarn through and complete dc in
usual way—called 1 double around back
(dc around Bk)—, now work *5 dc around

Ft, 5 dc around Bk, rep from * to within
last 5[2:4] sts, dc around Ft to end.
Turn.
2nd row 2 ch, work 4[1:3] dc around Bk,
5 dc around Ft, *5 dc around Bk, 5 dc
around Ft, rep from * to within last
5[2:4] sts, dc around Bk to end.
Turn.
3rd row As 1st row.
4th row As 1st row.
5th row As 2nd row.
6th row As 1st row.
These 6 rows form patt. Continue in patt.
until work measures 13¾[13¾:14¼]in
(35[35:36.5]cm) from beg, ending with
a WS row.
Divide for neck
Next row Patt 27[29:31] sts. Turn.
Complete this side first. Work one row.
Keeping armhole edge straight, work
2 dc tog at neck edge on next and then
every other row until 19[21:23] sts
rem. Work one row. Fasten off.
Return to other side, skip center st, join
yarn to next st, 2 ch, patt to end.
Complete the second side to match
the first side, but reverse shaping.
Waistband
Using No. 7 (5mm) needles and with RS
of work facing, pick up and K67[71:75]
sts evenly along lower edge.
1st row * K1, P1, rep from * to last st, K1.
2nd row K2, * P1, K1, rep from * to last
st, K1. Rep last 2 rows until waistband
measures 4in (10cm) from beg.

Bind off loosely in ribbing.
Back
Work as front, omitting neck shaping.
Waistband
Work as given for front waistband.

Sleeves

Using size K (7.00mm) hook make 36 ch
and work base row as for front, 35 sts.
Next row 2 ch, 4 dc around Ft, *5 dc
around Bk, 5 dc around Ft, rep from * to
end. Turn. Cont in patt as now set.
Work one row. Keeping patt correct,
inc one st at each end of next and
then every 3rd row until there are
49[49:52] sts. Cont without shaping
until sleeve measures 15¾in (40cm) from
beg. Fasten off.

Cuff

Using No. 7 (5mm) needles and with RS
of work facing, pick up and K 37 sts evenly
along lower edge. Work 3½in (9cm)
ribbing as for front. Bind off loosely in
ribbing.

87

To finish

Do not block. Place colored marker on 19th[21st:23rd] sts from each side edge on back. Join right shoulder seam from armhole edge to marker.

Neck border Using No. 7 (5mm) needles and with RS of work facing, pick up and K 45 sts evenly down left side of front neck (5 sts for each 2 rows), pick up and K one st from point of V and mark it with a colored thread, 45 sts up right side of neck and 29 sts evenly between markers at back of neck, 120 sts.

1st row *P1, K1, rep from * to within 2 sts of marked st, P2 tog, P1, P2 tog tbl, rib to end.

2nd row Rib to within 2 sts of marked st, K2 tog tbl, K1, K2 tog, rib to end. Work 5 more rows ribbing, dec in this way on every row. Bind off in ribbing, dec as before. Join left shoulder and neck border seam. Mark depth of armholes 9[9:9½] in (23[23:24]cm) from shoulder seams back and front and sew in sleeves. Then join side and sleeve seams.

Technique tip
Basket weave pattern

The basket weave pattern in this sweater is not nearly as complicated as it looks. The technique consists of working doubles around each other, instead of working them into the tops of the stitches in the preceding row, as you normally do. In this way, you form horizontal and vertical blocks of doubles. By alternating the placement of the blocks, you produce the basket weave effect. The number of stitches in a block may vary, in this sweater each block is five stitches across and three rows deep.

After completing your base row of doubles, turn the work and make two chains to count as first stitch. Wind yarn around hook and insert the hook between the first and second doubles, from front to back. Take hook behind the second double, then bring it to the front between second and third doubles.

Wind yarn around hook and draw it through. You now have three loops on hook. Complete the double in the usual way. This is called "double around front." Work around next three doubles in the same way. These first five stitches (counting the turning chain at edge) will form part of the first vertical block.

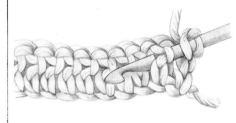

For the horizontal block the process is reversed; instead of inserting the hook from front to back, you insert it from the back of the work to the front. Wind yarn around hook and insert hook between fifth and sixth doubles of preceding row, from back to front, take hook over the sixth double, then insert it between sixth and seventh doubles from front to back. Wind yarn around hook, draw it through (three loops on hook), and complete the double in the usual way. This is called "double around back." Work around each of next four doubles in the same way. Continue across the row in this way, alternating the groups of horizontal and vertical stitches.

On the second row, reverse the sequence. That is, if you ended the previous row by working five doubles around front—as in our sample—work around these doubles by working doubles around back.

Thus, you are simultaneously working a horizontal block (viewed from one side) and a vertical one (viewed from the other). Similarly, your next group of stitches is worked using doubles around front. The sample below shows the second row completed.

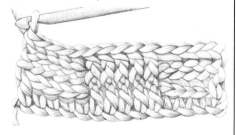

When you have completed the first row of blocks, i.e. three rows of doubles, alternate the order of the next row of blocks by working the following row of stitches in the same way as the previous row. Thus, if you finished that row with doubles around front, begin the next row with doubles around front to produce the alternating effect shown in the sample below.

The basket weave pattern produces a warm and highly textured fabric.

Shoestring

Knitting needle fold-away

This attractive folding case is just the thing to keep your needles in order while you are following our Knitting Course. You will be able to find the needle size you want at a glance and the slim-line design makes it easy to store.

Materials
2 pieces of fabric in contrasting colors, 20 x 18in (50 x 45cm)
Piece of lining fabric, 18 x 8¼in (45 x 21cm)
1⅜yd (1.2m) bias binding, 1in (2.5cm) wide
¾yd (.6m) of ⅝in (1.5cm)-wide cotton seam tape
Two small snap fasteners
9 pairs of knitting needles

1 Lay the knitting needles on the material you are using for the inside of the holder, parallel to the longer edge. Cut the bias binding into two 23½in (60cm) lengths. Pin and baste these pieces over the needles, one 6in (15cm) from the top edge, the other 8in (20cm) from the bottom. Remove the needles from the loops. Topstitch the bias binding in place, forming a rectangle of stitching between each needle loop. Trim off excess tapes at sides.

2 To reinforce the bottom edge of the holder (where the points of the needles will come), baste the piece of lining fabric to the wrong side of the cover material.

3 Lay the reinforced outer fabric on the inner fabric, right sides together. Baste and stitch around the edges, taking a ⅜in (1cm) seam, leaving the bottom edge unstitched. Make sure ends of bias binding are aligned with side edges.

4 Turn right side out and press, folding under and pressing ⅜in (1cm) along the bottom edge.

5 Topstitch across the bottom edge.

6 Turn 2¼in (6cm) of the bottom edge up toward the bias binding and then pin in place.

7 Topstitch around the remaining three sides of the holder to secure the turned-up edge.

8 Turn down 2in (5cm) of the top edge of the material and sew a snap in place on each side at the corners.

9 Fold the cotton tape in half widthwise, and make a crease along the fold. Sew the tape along the crease to the outside of the holder, about 1¼in (3.5cm) from the edge. Replace needles, roll up the holder and tie with the tape.

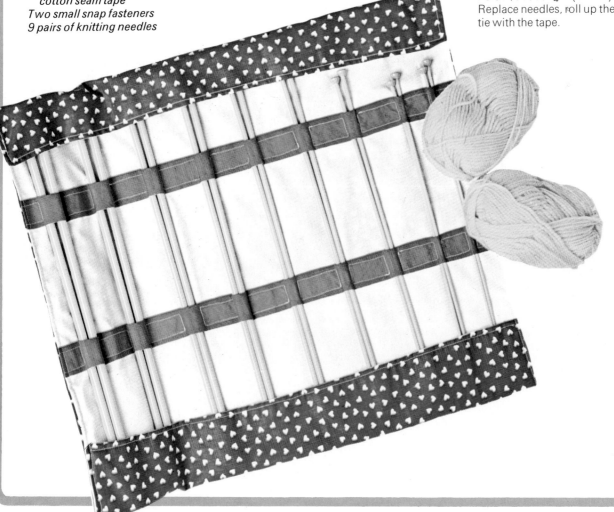

CROCHET

Woven crochet cardigan

This pretty check cardigan is made by weaving different colors through a striped filet background. The yarn used is a mixture of silk and wool.

Sizes

To fit 34[36:38]in (87[91:97]cm) bust.
Length, 21[21¾:22½]in (53[55:57]cm)
Sleeve seam, 17¾[18½:19¼]in (45[47:49]cm)

Note Directions for the larger sizes are in brackets []; where there is only one set of figures it applies to all sizes.

Note Measurements shown on the diagram on page 91 are before weaving. Weaving will make the crochet shorter and wider.

Gauge

10 sps and 10 rows to 4in (10cm) in patt worked on size H (5.00mm) hook.

Materials

14[15:15]oz (400[420:420]g) of wool/ silk sport yarn in main color (A)
7[8:8]oz (200[220:220]g) in contrasting color (B)
1 oz (20g) in each of two contrasting colors (C) and (D)
Size F (4.00mm) and size H (5.00mm) crochet hooks
8 buttons
1 long tapestry needle for weaving

Back

Using size F (4.00mm) hook and A, chain 23.

1st row 1 sc into 2nd ch from hook, 1 sc into each ch to end, turn. 22 sts.

2nd row 1 ch to count as first sc, working into back loop only of each st, work 1 sc into each st to end, turn. Rep 2nd row 88[92:96] times more to complete ribbing.

Beg patt as foll: Turn ribbing sideways. Using size H (5.00mm) hook, cont working along side edge of ribbing.

Next row Using A, 4 ch to count as first dc and 1-ch sp, 1 dc into top of 2nd row end, *1 ch, skip 1 row end, 1 dc into top of next row end, rep from * to end of ribbing, working last dc into edge of last row end. 45[47:49] 1-ch sps.

2nd row Using A, 4 ch to count as first dc and 1-ch sp, 1dc into next dc, *1 ch, 1 dc into next dc, rep from * to end of row working last dc into 3rd of first 4 ch and joining in C at end of row, turn.

3rd row Using C, 1 ch to count as first sc,

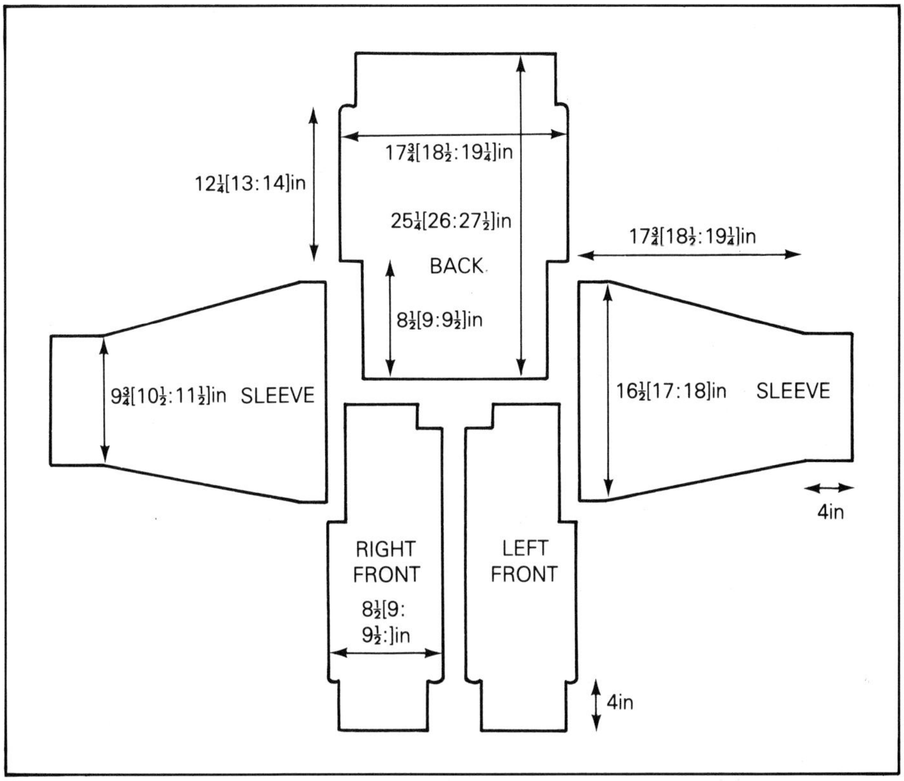
12¼[13:14]in
17¾[18½:19¼]in
25¼[26:27½]in
BACK
8½[9:9½]in
17¾[18½:19¼]in
9¾[10½:11½]in SLEEVE
16½[17:18]in SLEEVE
4in
RIGHT FRONT
LEFT FRONT
8½[9:
9½:]in
4in

John Hutchinson

*1 sc into next 1-ch sp, 1 sc into next dc, rep from * to end of row, working last sc into 3rd of 4 ch and changing to A at end of row, turn.

4th row Using A, 4 ch to count as first dc and 1-ch sp, skip next sc, 1dc into next sc, *1 ch, skip one sc, 1dc into next sc, rep from * to end of row, working last dc into first ch, turn.

5th-16th rows Work as for 2nd row, working in color sequence of 1 row A, 1 row B, 1 row A, 2 rows B, 1 row A, 2 rows B, 1 row A, 1 row B, 2 rows A.

17th row Using D, as 3rd row.

4th-17th rows form patt and are rep throughout noting that B and C are used alternately when sc row is reached. Cont working in patt and color sequence until 31[33:35] rows in all have been worked from waistband. Fasten off.

Shape armholes

Next row With RS of work facing, rejoin correct color in sequence to 9th[11th:11th] st from side edge, patt to last 8[10:10] sts, turn and leave rem sts unworked.

Cont working in patt and color sequence on rem sts for 22[23:24] rows. Fasten off.

Right front

Using size F (4.00mm) hook and A, chain 23. Work 45[47:49] rows rib as for back waistband. Beg patt as foll:

Using size H (5.00mm) hook and A, turn ribbing and work in patt as for back across edge of ribbing. 22[23:24] 1-ch sps.

Cont in patt as for back until 31[33:35] rows have been worked from waistband.

Shape armholes

Next row Patt to last 8[10:10] sts, turn and leave rem sts unworked.

Cont in patt on these sts for 14 rows. Fasten off.

Shape neck

Next row With RS of work facing, rejoin correct color to 10th[10th:12th] st, at front edge, counting each dc and each 1-ch sp as one st, patt to end.

Cont in patt on rem sts, work 7[8:9] rows from beg of neck shaping. Fasten off.

Left front

Work as for right front, reversing armhole and neck shaping.

Sleeves

Using size F (4.00mm) hook and A chain 23. Work in rib as for back for 45[49:53] rows. Beg patt as foll:

Turn ribbing sideways. Using size H (5.00mm) hook, cont working along side edge of ribbing.

Next row Using A, 4 ch to count as first dc and 1-ch sp, 1 dc into first row end, 1 ch, (1 dc into next row end, 1 ch) twice, skip next row end, *1 dc into next row end, 1 ch, skip next row end, rep from * to last 3 rows ends, (1 dc into next row end, 1 ch) twice, 1 dc into last row end, turn. 51[57:59] sts and 25[27:29] 1-ch sps.

Cont in st and color patt starting from 4th row of color sequence as for back, using C for first sc stripe and inc one sp at each end of every 4th row by working (1 dc, 1 ch) into first space at beg of row and (1 ch, 1 dc) into last sp at end of row, until there are 83[87:91] sts and 41[43:45] 1-ch sps. Cont in patt until 45[47:49] rows have been worked from cuff. Fasten off.

Neckband

Using size F (4.00mm) hook and A, chain 8. Work in rib as for back until strip measures 13[13¾:14½]in (33[35:37]cm). Fasten off.

To finish

Weave each piece before it is sewn together. Work weaving vertically with the yarn used double, working 2 lines of weaving into each chain space.

Measure length of yarn needed for each vertical row, plus 8in (20cm), then cut several lengths at once. When weaving, leave a loop of 2½in (6cm) at edge so that fabric and checks can be adjusted once weaving has been completed.

Weaving sleeves

Using C, start at cuff and center 1-ch sp of sleeve. Weave in and out of each 1-ch sp to top of sleeve. Work another line of weaving into same 1-ch sp (2 lines of weaving up center of sleeve). Cont working each side of center, working 2 lines of weaving into each vertical row of 1-ch sps and using colors as foll: 2 lines A, 1 line B, 1 line A, 2 lines B, 1 line A, 1 line B, 2 lines A, 1 line D, cont weaving to side of sleeve on each side of center stripe in this way, noting that you should alternate C and D when they occur in weaving as in crochet stripe patt.

Weaving back and fronts

Join shoulder seams. Beg at center space at center of back and using C double work 2 lines weaving from rib to top of back. Using yarn double throughout and working 2 lines of weaving up each vertical row of 1-ch sps, work weaving in color sequence as given for sleeve, working from center back to either side and working back and fronts tog by taking weaving across shoulder seam and down fronts to waistband.

Set in sleeves along straight edge. Join sleeve and side seams, working from cuff, up sleeve, along bodice to waistband. Sew neckband in place.

Button band

Using size F (4.00mm) hook and A, work as for neck edging until strip is long enough to fit from neck to hem, slightly stretched. Sew to left front.

Buttonhole band

Mark position for 7 buttons on button band, first to come ¾[1¼:1½]in (2[3:4]cm) from beg, with 7 more at 2½in (6cm) intervals up band. Work buttonhole band as for button band, making buttonholes as markers are reached as foll:

Next row 1 ch, 1 sc into back loop of next st, 3 ch, skip next 3 sts, 1 sc into back loop of each st to end, turn.

Next row Work in sc, working into back loop of each st and working 1 sc into each ch made in previous row, turn.

Sew buttonhole band to right front. Sew on buttons to correspond.

Many a slip

An overall slip stitch pattern in soft pastel colors adds interest to the front of this trim vest. Fasten the belt at the front or back, whichever you prefer.

Sizes

To fit 32[34:36:38:40]in (83[87:92:97:102]cm) bust. Length, 21¼[21½:21¾:22:22¼]in (53.5[54:54.5:55.5:56]cm). **Note** Directions for the larger sizes are in brackets []; where there is only one set of figures it applies to all sizes.

Materials

7[7:8:8:9]oz (200[200:225:225: 250]g) of a fingering yarn
1[1:2:2:2]oz (25[25:50:50:50]g) each of contrasting colors (B, C and D)
1 pair each Nos. 2 and 3 (3 and 3¼mm) knitting needles
5 buttons
Slide buckle, ¾in (2cm) with 1½in (4cm) bar

Gauge

30 sts to 4in (10cm) over sl st patt on No. 3 (3¼mm) needles.
30 sts and 39 rows to 4in (10cm) over ribbing, when slightly stretched, on No. 3 (3¼mm) needles.

Back

Using No. 3 (3¼mm) needles and A, cast on 129[135:143:151:159] sts.
1st row K1, *P1, K1, rep from * to end.
2nd row P1, *K1, P1, rep from * to end.
These 2 rows form ribbing patt and are rep throughout. Cont until work measures 3in (7.5cm) from beg. Mark each end of last row. Change to No. 2 (3mm) needles and work a further 2in (5cm) in ribbing. Mark each end of last row. Change to No. 3 (3¼mm) needles. Cont in ribbing until work measures 12in (30.5cm) from beg. Mark each end of last row with a colored thread to denote beg of armholes. Cont in ribbing until armholes measure 8¼[8½:8¾:9:9¼]in (21[21.5:22:23:23.5]cm).

Shape shoulders

Binding off in ribbing, bind off 8[8:8:9:9] sts at beg of next 6 rows and 7[8:10:10:12] sts at beg of foll 4 rows. Bind off rem 53[55:55:57:57] sts.

Left front

Using No. 3 (3¼mm) needles and A, cast on 58[62:66:70:74] sts. Work 7 rows K1, P1, ribbing. P1 row. Beg patt. Slip sts with yarn at back on K rows and at front on P rows.
1st row (RS) Using B, K1, *sl2, K4, rep from * to last 3[1:5:3:1] sts, sl2, K1[K1:sl2, K3:sl2, K1:K1].
2nd row Using B, P all knitted sts and sl all slipped sts in previous row.
3rd row Using C, K3, *sl2, K4, rep from * to last 1[5:3:1:5] sts, K1[sl2, K3:sl2, K1:K1:sl2, K3].
4th row Using C, as 2nd.
5th row Using D, K1, *K4, sl2, rep from * to last 3[1:5:3:1] sts, K3[1:5:3:1].
6th row Using D, as 2nd.
7th and 8th rows Using A, as 1st and 2nd.
9th and 10th rows Using B, as 3rd and 4th.
11th and 12th rows Using C, as 5th and 6th.
13th and 14th rows Using D, as 1st and 2nd.
15th and 16th rows Using A, as 3rd and 4th.
17th and 18th rows Using B, as 5th and 6th.
19th and 20th rows Using C, as 1st and 2nd.
21st and 22nd rows Using D, as 3rd and 4th.
23rd and 24th rows Using A, as 5th and 6th.
These 24 rows form patt and are repeated throughout. Cont in patt until work measures 3in (7.5cm). Mark side edge of last row with a colored thread. Change to No. 2 (3mm) needles. Work 2in (5cm) in patt. Mark side edge of last row. Change to No. 3 (3¼mm) needles. Cont in patt until front matches back to armhole. Mark both ends of last row.

Shape front edge

Keeping patt correct, dec one st at front edge on next and every 4th row until 38[40:44:47:51] sts rem. Cont without shaping until front matches back to shoulder, ending at side edge.

Shape shoulder

Bind off 8[8:8:9:9] sts at beg of next and foll 2 alternate rows and 7[8:10:10:12] sts at beg of foll alternate row. Work 1 row. Bind off.

Right front

Work as for left front, reversing shaping.

Right front band and collar

Using No. 2 (3mm) needles and A, cast on 12 sts. Work ½in (1cm) K1, P1 ribbing.
1st buttonhole row Rib 4, bind off 3 sts, rib to end.
2nd buttonhole row Rib to end, casting on 3 sts pver those bound off in previous row. Cont in ribbing, working a further 4 buttonholes at intervals of 2¾in (7cm). Cont in ribbing, inc one st at inside edge of next and every alternate row until there are 30 sts, then on every 3rd row until there are 36 sts. Cont straight until collar measures 12¼[12¾:13:13½:13¾]in (31[32.5:33:34.5:35]cm) from last buttonhole. Bind off in ribbing.

Left front band and collar

Work as for right band and collar; omit buttonholes and reverse shaping.

Belt (make 2)

Using No. 2 (3mm) needles and A, cast on 12 sts. Work 9½[10:10½:11:11½]in (24[25.5:26.5:28:29.5]cm) K1, P1 ribbing. Bind off in ribbing.

Armbands (alike)

Join shoulder seams. Using No. 2 (3mm) needles, A and with RS of work facing, pick up and K 128[134:140:146:152] sts between colored markers. Work 8 rows K1, P1 ribbing. Bind off in ribbing.

To finish

Press or block the work, depending on yarn used.

Join side seams, setting belt between waist markers at sides.

Join center back of collar. Sew on front bands and collar, matching beg of collar shaping to colored markers at start of front edge shaping. Press seams. Sew on buttons, Sew on buckle. Fasten buckle at front or back.

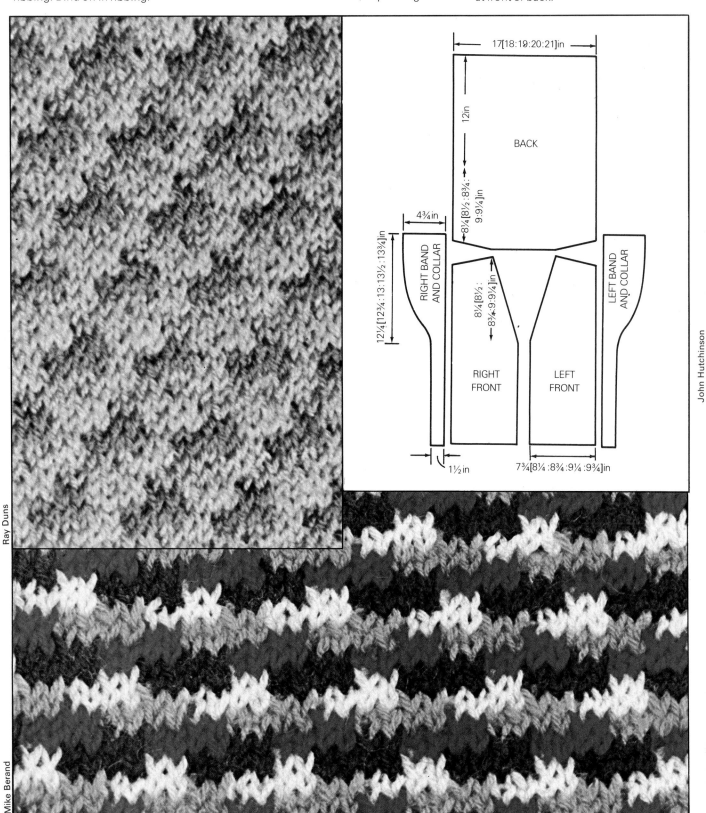

94

Working slip stitch patterns

Slip stitch patterns – like colorwork designs – have a complex, multi-colored appearance, but they are much easier to work. Whereas in colorwork knitting two colors are alternated within a single row by carrying the yarns across the back of the work, in slip stitch patterns only one color is used in a row. For the beginner they make an easy introduction to colored patterns, offering an interesting range of color and design possibilities with fewer difficulties in regulating stitch gauge than are to be found in colorwork knitting.

Initially, it is best to practice with yarns of a similar weight, concentrating on the design scope of the colors themselves. Later on, you'll enjoy experimenting with varying textures and types of yarn. The step-by-step sequence illustrates the techniques used in slip stitch designs, particularly as they apply to the pattern of the vest shown on page 92. For our sample we have used only two colors, instead of four. Compare the finished result using two colors (see step 5) with that of the vest, which uses four.

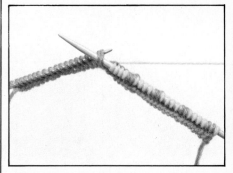

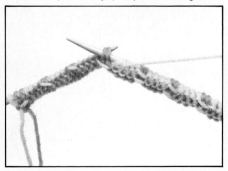

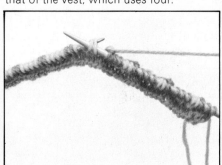

1 Cast on a multiple of six stitches plus two extra stitches, using one of the colors (A). Purl one row. Join in the second color (B) and using B work the first pattern row: K1, *sl 2, K4, rep from * to last st, K1. This knit row is the right side of the fabric. When slipping stitches on right-side rows, keep the yarn at the back and slip them purlwise from left-hand to right-hand needle.

2 The 2nd row and all other wrong-side rows are worked in the same way. Use the same color as the previous row (here it is B) and purl all the stitches that were knitted in B in the previous row. Slip all the stitches in color A again; keep the yarn at the front (wrong side) of the work when slipping stitches and slip them purlwise.

3 Return to color A to work the 3rd row. K3, *sl 2, K4, rep from * to last 5 sts, sl 2, K3. Note that you are now knitting all the stitches in A that were slipped during the previous two rows. The stitches being slipped in this row are in B.

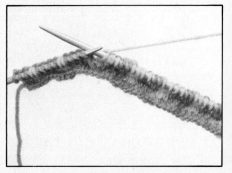

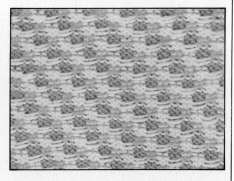

4 Work a wrong-side row, then use B to work the 5th row. K1, *K4, sl 2, rep from * to last st, K1. The slipped stitches are drawn into and become part of the row you are working, so giving a two-color effect even though you are only using a single ball of yarn. Purl another row to complete six rows.

5 Repeat the six pattern rows throughout, alternating colors A and B every two rows, to create a diagonal staggered check effect.

6 On the wrong side of the sample of fabric are horizontal strands of yarn where they have been carried across slipped stitches.

Mike Berend

EXTRA SPECIAL KNITTING

Wrapping up baby

Get the hang of lace knitting by making this beautiful baby's blanket. The pattern is typical of the kind of knitting originating in the Shetland Isles, so you'll be creating an heirloom with a truly traditional feel.

Kim Sayer

96

Size
46in (117cm) square.

Gauge
1 patt rep (18 sts) to 4in (10cm)
No. 6 (4½mm) needles.

Materials
16oz (450g) of a sport yarn
1 pair of No. 6 (4½mm) needles

Blanket center
Cast on 217 sts. Begin patt noting that sts are added on right side (RS) rows and reduced to the original number on wrong side (WS) rows.
1st row (RS) K2, *yo, K1, yo, sl 1, K1, psso, K9, K2 tog, yo, K1, yo, K3 rep from * to end, but finish last rep K2 instead of K3. 241 sts.
2nd row P5, *P2 tog, P7, P2 tog through back of loops (tbl), P9, rep from * to end, but finish last rep P5 instead of P9. 217 sts.
3rd row K2, yo, K3, yo, sl 1, K1, psso, K5, K2 tog, *(yo, K3) 3 times, yo, sl 1, K1, psso, K5, K2 tog, rep from * to last 5 sts, yo, K3, yo, K2. 241 sts.
4th row P7, *P2 tog, P3, P2 tog tbl, P13, rep from * to end, but finish last rep P7. 217 sts.
5th row K2, *yo, K5, yo, sl 1, K1, psso, K1, K2 tog, yo, K5, yo, K3, rep from * to end, but finish last rep K2. 241 sts.
6th row P9, *P3 tog, P17, rep from * to end, but finish last rep P9. 217 sts.
7th row K5, *K2 tog, yo, K1, yo, K3, yo, K1, yo, sl 1, K1, psso, K9, rep from * to end, but finish last rep K5. 241 sts.
8th row P4, *P2 tog tbl, P9, P2 tog, P7, rep from * to end, but finish last rep P4. 217 sts.
9th row K3, *K2 tog, (yo, K3) 3 times, yo, sl 1, K1, psso, K5, rep from * to end, but finish last rep K3, 241 sts.
10th row P2, *P2 tog tbl, P13, P2 tog. P3, rep from * to end, but finish last rep P2. 217 sts.
11th row K1, *K2 tog, yo, K5, yo, K3, yo, K5, yo, sl 1, K1, psso, K1, rep from * to end. 241 sts.
12th row P2 tog, *P17, P3 tog, rep from * to end, but finish last rep P2 tog. 217 sts.
These 12 rows form the patt. Rep them 23 times more. Bind off.

Edging
Cast on 9 sts. K1 row and P1 row. Begin patt.
1st row (RS) Sl 1, K2, yo, K2 tog tbl, K2 tbl, pick up loop lying between sts and K tbl – called M1 –, K2 tbl. 10 sts.
2nd row K2 tbl, P1, P2 tbl, K2, yo, K2 tog tbl, P1. 10 sts.
3rd row Sl 1, K2, yo, K2 tog tbl, K3 tbl, M1, K2 tbl. 11 sts.
4th row K2 tbl, P1, P3 tbl, K2, yo, K2

Technique tips
The lace pattern
Knitting lace patterns involves increasing stitches by one of the methods of decorative increasing – in this pattern the method is bringing the yarn forward and over the needle (yo) before knitting the next stitch to increase a stitch and make a hole. The increased stitches – say three in each pattern repeat across the row – must be compensated for by decreasing an equal number immediately or in the next row. The first method is to bring the yarn forward and slip the next stitch from the left-hand to the right-hand needle. Knit the next stitch; then, with the left needle, pass the slipped stitch over the knitted one, as shown. This decrease compensates for the increase made when bringing the yarn forward and over the needle. The abbreviation for this process is: "yo, sl 1, K1, psso."

In this pattern you will more often use the second method of making a hole: bring the yarn forward and over the needle to make an extra stitch, and knit the next stitch from the LH needle.

On the next row, work the extra (yo) stitch along with the next stitch to decrease one stitch, thus ending with the same number of stitches you started with.

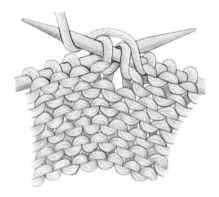

The finished effect of the increase and decrease is a small hole.

Finishing method for lace blanket or shawl
This type of blanket does not need pressing; instead it is dampened and stretched. First roll it in a damp cloth, then spread it on a sheet on the floor over a carpet and pin the opposite corners. Pin along the sides, placing a pin through each point of the lace border. Keep the blanket taut and square until it is completely dry.

tog tbl, P1. 11 sts.
5th row Sl 1, K2, yo, K2 tog tbl, K4 tbl, M1, K2 tbl. 12 sts.
6th row K2 tbl, P1, P4 tbl, K2, yo, K2 tog tbl, P1. 12 sts.
7th row Sl 1, K2, yo, K2 tog tbl, K5 tbl, M1, K2 tbl. 13 sts.
8th row K2 tbl, P1, P5 tbl, K2, yo, K2 tog tbl, P1. 13 sts.
9th row Sl 1, K2, yo, K2 tog tbl, K6 tbl, M1, K2 tbl. 14 sts.
10th row K2 tbl, P1, P6 tbl, K2, yo, K2 tog tbl, P1. 14 sts.
11th row Sl 1, K2, yo, K2 tog tbl, K7 tbl, M1, K2 tbl. 15 sts.
12th row K2 tbl, P1, P7 tbl, K2, yo, K2 tog tbl, P1. 15 sts.

13th row Sl 1, K2, yo, K2 tog tbl, K10 tbl. 15 sts.
14th row K10 tbl, K2, yo, K2 tog tbl, P1. 15 sts.
15th row As 13th row.
16th row Bind off 6, K1 tbl, P1, P1 tbl, K2, yo, K2 tog tbl, P1. 9 sts. These 16 rows form the patt. Rep them until edging fits outer edge of blanket center allowing an extra 1½in (4cm) at each corner, ending with a 16th row. Bind off.

To finish
Join cast-on and bound-off edges of edging together. Sew edging to main piece easing it in at corners. Finish as described in Technique tips (above).

EXTRA SPECIAL KNITTING

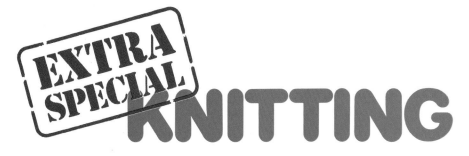

Family Fair Isle sweaters

This traditional design for a Fair Isle sweater can be made in sizes for all the family. The band of pattern looks equally attractive in subtle natural shades or in bright rainbow colors.

Sizes
To fit 26[28:30:32:34:36:38:40:42:44:46]in (66[71:76:81:86:91:97:102:107:112:117]cm) bust/chest.
Length, 19¾[20¼:20½:23¾:24:24½:24½:25:27½:27¾:27¾]in (50[51:52:60:61:62:62:63:70:71:71]cm).
Sleeve seam, 12¾[12¾:12¾:15½:15½:15½:15½:15½:18:18:18]in (32[32:32:39:39:39:39:39:46:46:46]cm).
Note Directions for the larger sizes are in brackets []; where there is only one set of figures it applies to all sizes.

Gauge
18 sts and 17 rows to 4in (10cm) in Fair Isle patt chart I on No. 9 (5½mm) needles.

Materials
7[7:7:8:8:8:9:9:9:10:10] 3½oz (100g) skeins of a bulky knitting yarn in main color (A)
1[1:1:1:2:2:2:2:3:3] skeins in contrasting colors (B) and (C)
1 skein in contrasting color (D)
One pair each No. 7 (4½mm) and No. 9 (5½mm) knitting needles
1 ball thinner yarn matching main color

Back
Using No. 7 (4½mm) needles and A, cast on 64[68:72:76:80:88:92:96:100:104:108] sts. Work in K2, P2 rib for 2in (5cm), inc 1 st at each end of last row. 66[70:74:78:82:90:94:98:102:106:110] sts.
Change to No. 9 (5½mm) needles and beg Fair Isle patt chart I. Cont in this way until back measures approx 10¾[10¾:10¾:13½:13½:13½:13½:13½:16:16:16]in (27[27:27:34:34:34:34:34:41:41:41]cm) from beg, ending with a 12th patt row. Change to Fair Isle chart II and work 2in (5cm) more, ending with a P row.
Shape armholes
Keeping continuity of Fair Isle patt, bind off 4[4:4:5:5:5:6:6:7:7:8] sts at beg of next

□ = A ● = B X = C ○ = D

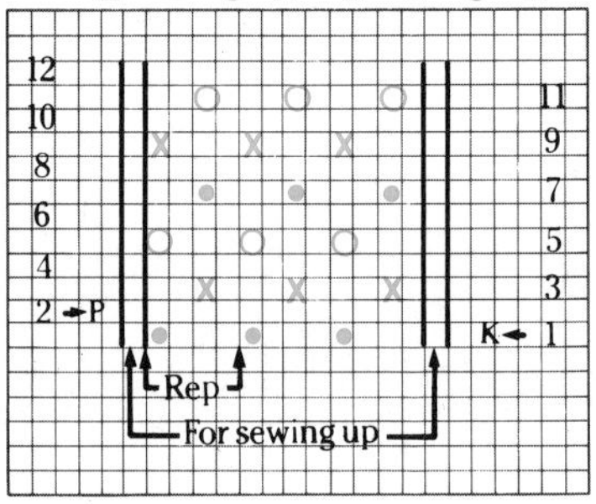

CHART I

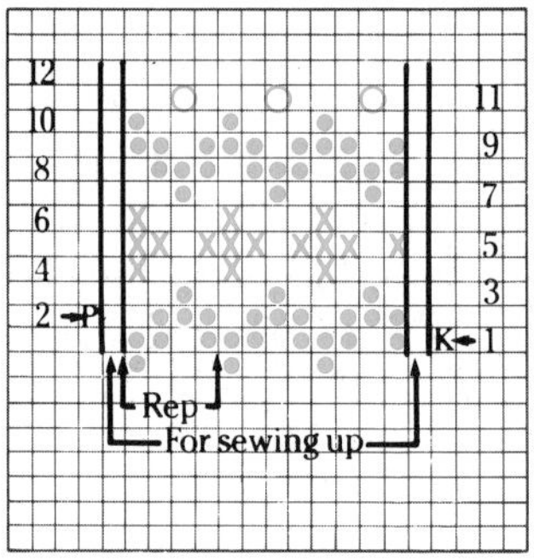

CHART II

2 rows. Dec 1 st at each end of the next and every other row until 52[56:60:64:68:72:72:76:76:80:80] sts rem, ending with a P row. Cont in patt until armholes measure 5[5:6:6:6:6¼:6¾:6¾:6¾:6¾]in (13[13:15:15:15:16:16:17:17:17:17]cm) from beg of shaping, ending with a P row.
Shape neck
Patt 20[22:22:25:27:29:29:29:29:31:31] sts and turn, leaving rem sts on a spare needle. Dec 1 st at neck edge on every row until 17[18:19:21:22:22:24:25:26:26:27] sts rem. Cont even until armholes measure 7[7½:7¾:8¼:8½:9:9:9½:9½:9¾:9¾]in (18[19:20:21:22:23:23:24:24:25:25]cm) from beg of shaping, ending at armhole edge.
Shape shoulders
Bind off 6[6:6:7:7:7:8:8:9:9:9] sts at shoulder edge twice. Work 1 row.
Bind off rem 5[6:7:7:8:8:8:9:8:8:9] sts.
With RS facing, return to sts on spare needle, slip center 12[12:16:14:14:14:14:18:18:18:18] sts onto a st holder.
Join in yarn to next st, patt to end.
Now complete to match first side of neck, reversing all shaping.

Front
Work as for back.

Sleeves
Using No. 7 (4½mm) needles and A, cast on 32[36:36:36:36:40:40:44:44:48:48] sts.
Work in K2, P2 rib for 2in (5cm), inc 1 st at each end of last row. 34[38:38:38:38:42:42:46:46:50:50] sts.
Change to No. 9 (5½mm) needles and beg Fair Isle chart I.
Work in patt, inc 1 st at each end of 2nd[2nd:2nd:6th:6th:6th:6th:6th:6th:6th:6th] row and then every 4th[4th:3rd:4th:3rd:4th:3rd:3rd:4th:4th:4th] row until there are 50[54:58:58:62:62:66:70:70:74:74] sts.
When sleeve measures approx 10¾[10¾:10¾:13½:13½:13½:13½:13½:16:16:16]in (27[27:27:34:34:34:34:34:41:41:41]cm) from cast-on edge, ending with a 12th patt row, change to Fair Isle chart II and work 2in (5cm) more, ending with a P row.
Shape cap
Bind off 4[4:4:5:5:5:6:6:7:7:8] sts at the beg of next 2 rows.
Decrease 1 st at each end of next and every other row until 34[38:40:36:40:38:42:40:36:42:38] sts remain, then dec 1 st at each end of every row until 14[14:16:16:16:18:18:20:20:22:22] sts remain.
Bind off.

To finish
Using thinner matching yarn, join right shoulder seam
Neckband
With RS of work facing, using No. 7 (4½mm) needles and A, pick up and K11[13:11:13:13:15:16:15:15:17:17] sts down left side of front neck, K12[12:16:14:14:14:14:18:18:18:18] sts from front

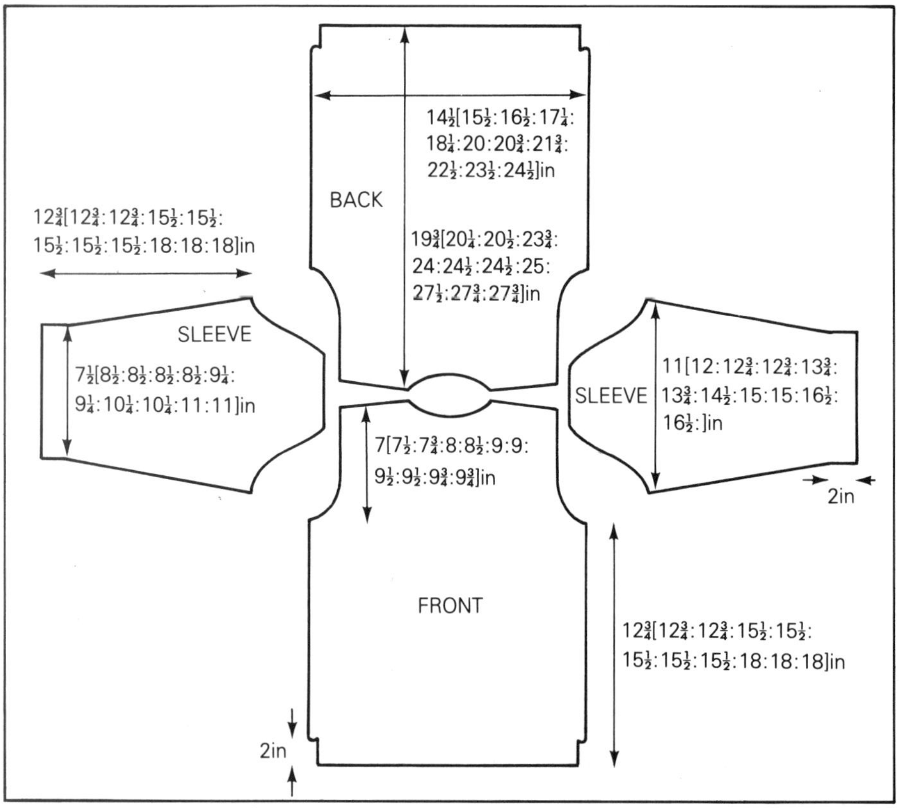
BACK
14½[15½:16½:17¼:
18¼:20:20¾:21¾:
22½:23½:24½]in
19¾[20¼:20½:23¾:
24:24½:24½:25:
27½:27¾:27¾]in
12¾[12¾:12¾:15½:15½:
15½:15½:15½:18:18:18]in
SLEEVE
7½[8½:8½:8½:8½:9¼:
9¼:10¼:10¼:11:11]in
7[7½:7¾:8:8½:9:9:
9½:9½:9¾:9¾]in
SLEEVE
11[12:12¾:12¾:13¾:
13¾:14½:15:15:16½:
16½:]in
2in
FRONT
12¾[12¾:12¾:15½:15½:
15½:15½:15½:18:18:18]in
2in

John Hutchinson

st holder, pick up and K11[13:11:13:13:15:16:15:15:17:17] sts up right side of front neck, 11[13:11:13:13:15:16:15:15:17:17] sts down right side of back neck, K12[12:16:14:14:14:14:18:18:18:18] sts from back st holder, pick up and K11[13:11:13:13:15:16:15:15:17:17] sts up left side of back neck. 68[76:76:80:80:88:92:96:96:104:104] sts. Work 4in (10cm) in K2, P2 rib. Bind off loosely in rib.

Press on WS using a warm iron (wool setting) over a damp cloth skipping ribbing.

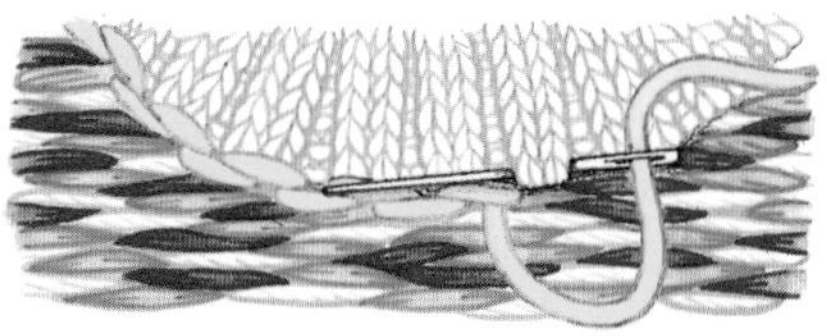

Using thinner matching yarn, join left shoulder, neckband, side and sleeve seams.

Fold neckband in half to WS and sew down with herringbone stitch as shown in picture above.

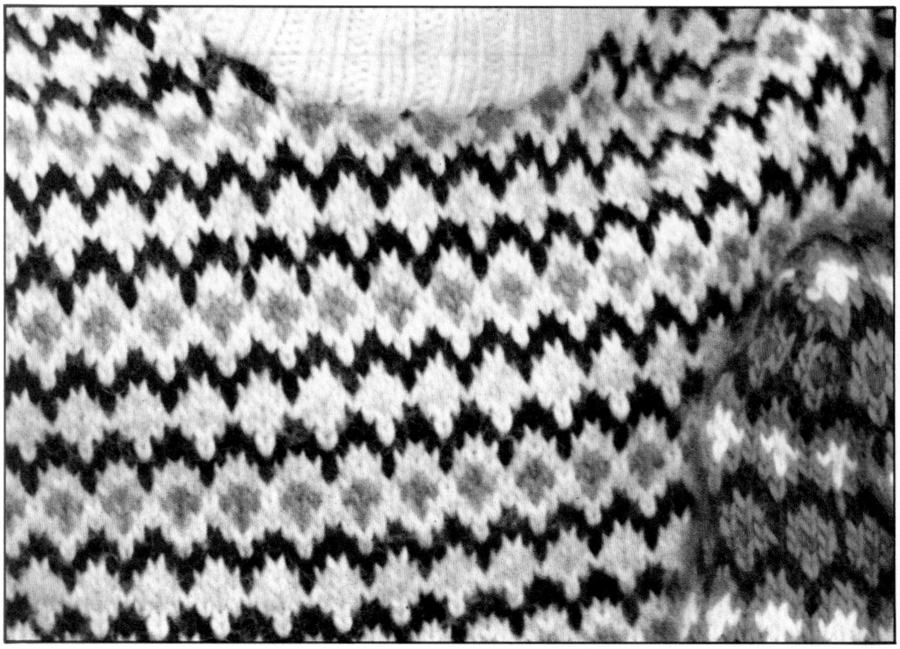

Roger Eaton

Technique tip

Carrying yarn

When using two colors or more, the yarn color not in use passes in loose strands across the back of the work behind the contrasting stitches until it is needed again. Be careful not to pull the color not in use too tight on the wrong side of the work, which causes puckering.

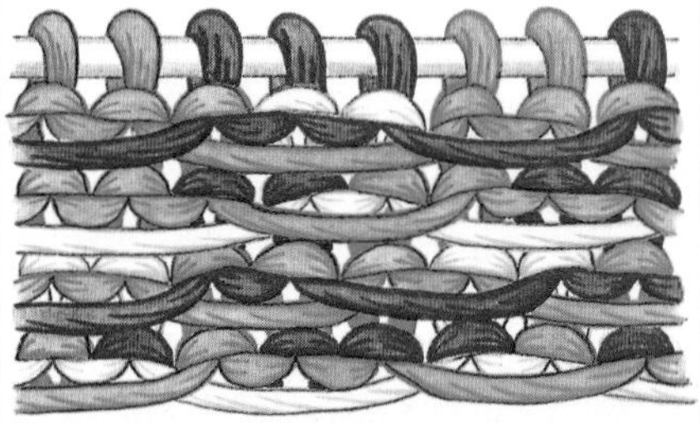

When only two colors are used in each row, it is possible to control one with each hand. If you are right-handed you will probably prefer to use this hand to control the most often-used color.

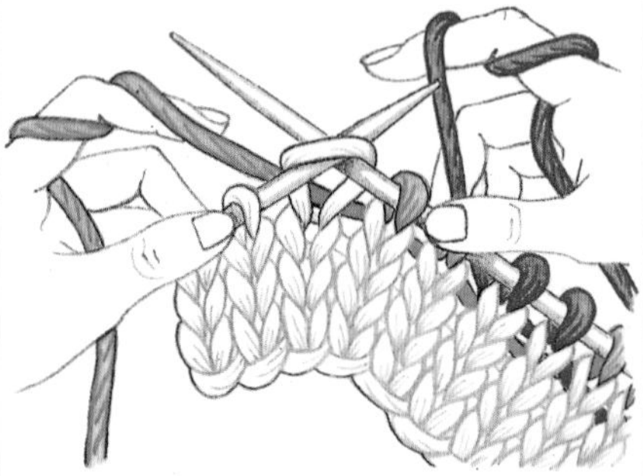

When the right-hand color is being used, the left hand holds the other color out of the way. When the lefthand color is being used, the right hand holds the other contrast color.

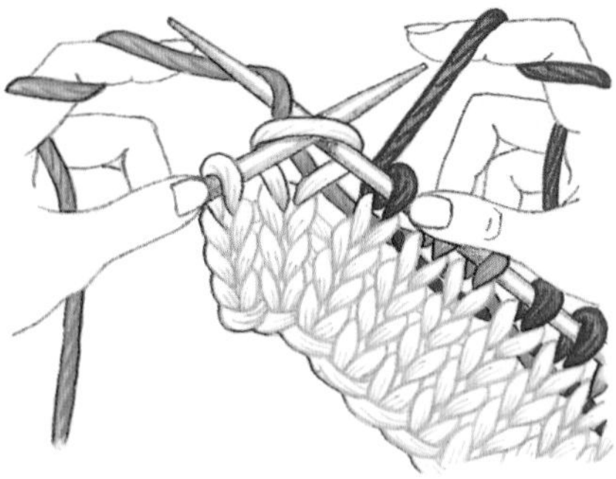

Coral Mula

These diagrams show carrying at the back of the work on a knit row. On a purl row the carrying is worked at the front.

KNITTING

Arans for the children

Two brightly colored Arans—with handy zip-up pockets—to make. These warm hard-wearing jackets will be firm favorites with the children.

Sizes
Chest 24[26:28:30]in (61[66:71:76]cm)
Length 14[15½:17:18½]in (36[39:43:47]cm).
Sleeve seam, 11[12½:14:15½]in (28[31.5:35.5:39.5]cm).
Note: Figures in brackets refer to larger sizes.

Jacket with neckband 13[15:16:18]oz (350[400:450:500]g) fingering yarn
Jacket with collar 13[15:15:16]oz (350[400:400:450]g) yarn
1 pair No. 3 (3¼mm) and No. 6 (4½mm) needles; cable needle
14[14:16:18]in (36[36:41:46]cm) open-ended zipper; three 4in (10cm) zippers for jacket with neckband

Gauge
20 sts and 28 rows to 4in (10cm) in reverse stockinette st on No. 6 (4½mm) needles.

Jacket with neckband
Back
Using No. 3 (3¼mm) needles cast on 63[67:71:75] sts.
1st row K1, (P1, K1) to end.
2nd row P1 (K1, P1) to end.
Rep these 2 rows 8 times more.
Next row Rib to end, inc 11 sts evenly across the row. 74[78:82:86] sts.
Change to No. 6 (4½mm) needles.
Next row K4[6:8:10], *P5, (K6, P5) twice *, K2, P8, K2, rep from * to * once, K4[6:8:10]. Begin patt.
1st row right side (RS) P4[6:8:10], *K2, into next st work K1, (wyif, K1) twice, turn; K5, turn; P5, turn; K1, sl1, K2 tog, psso, K1, turn; K3 tog—called make bobble or MB—, K2, P6, place next 2 sts on cable needle and leave at front of work, K2, P1, then K the sts from cable needle—called cross 5 or Cr5—, P6, K2, MB, K2*, P2, place next 2 sts on cable needle and leave at front of work, K2, then K the sts from cable needle—called cable 4 front or C4F—, place next 2 sts on cable needle and leave at back of work, K2, then K the sts from cable needle—called cable 4 back or C4B—, P2, rep from * to * once, P4[6:8:10].
2nd row K4[6:8:10], *P5, K6, P2, K1, P2, K6, P5 *, K2, P8, K2, rep from * to * once, K4[6:8:10].
3rd row P4[6:8:10], *K5, P5, place next st on cable needle and leave at back of

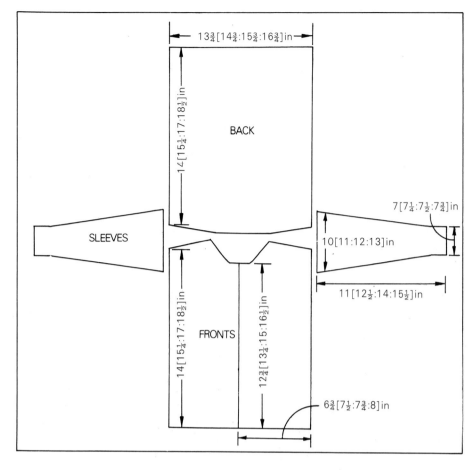

Back diagram with measurements: 13¾[14¾:15¾:16¾]in (top width), 14[15¼:17:18½]in (side height), BACK, 10[11:12:13]in, 7[7¼:7½:7¾]in, SLEEVES, FRONTS, 14[15¼:17:18½]in, 12¾[13¼:15:16½]in, 11[12½:14:15½]in, 6¾[7½:7¾:8]in

work, K2, then P the st from cable needle
—called cross 3 right or Cr3R—, K1, place
next 2 sts on cable needle and leave at
front of work, P1, then K the sts from
cable needle—called cross 3 left or Cr3L—,
P5, K5 *, P2, K8, P2, rep from * to *
once, P4[6:8:10].

4th row K4[6:8:10], *P5, K5, P2, K1,
P1, K1, P2, K5, P5 *, K2, P8, K2, rep from
* to * once, K4[6:8:10].

5th row P4[6:8:10], * K5, P4, Cr3R, K1,
P1, K1, Cr3L, P4, K5 *, P2, K8, P2, rep
from * to * once, P4[6:8:10].

6th row K4[6:8:10], * P5, K4, P2,
(K1, P1) 3 times, P1, K4, P5 *, K2, P8, K2,
rep from * to * once, K4[6:8:10].

7th row P4[6:8:10], * K2, MB, K2, P3,
Cr3R, K1, (P1, K1) twice, Cr3L, P3, K2,
MB, K2 *, P2, C4F, C4B, P2, rep from *
to * once, P4[6:8:10].

8th row K4[6:8:10], *P5, K3, P2, (K1,
P1) 4 times, P1, K3, P5 *, K2, P8, K2,
rep from * to * once, K4[6:8:10].

9th row P4[6:8:10], * K5, P2, Cr3R, K1,
(P1, K1) 3 times, Cr3L, P2, K5 *, P2, K8,
P2, rep from * to * once, P4[6:8:10].

10th row K4[6:8:10], * P5, K2, P2, (K1,
P1) 5 times, P1, K2, P5 *, K2, P8, K2,
rep from * to * once, K4[6:8:10].

11th row P4[6:8:10], * K5, P2, Cr3L, P1,
(K1, P1) 3 times, Cr3R, P2, K5 *, P2, K8,
P2, rep from * to * once, P4[6:8:10].

12th row As 8th row.

13th row P4[6:8:10], * K2, MB, K2, P3,
Cr3L, P1, (K1, P1) twice, Cr3R, P3, K2,
MB, K2 *, P2, C4F, C4B, P2, rep from *

to * once, P4[6:8:10].

14th row As 6th row.

15th row P4[6:8:10], * K5, P4, Cr3L, P1,
K1, P1, Cr3R, P4, K5 *, P2, K8, P2, rep
from * to * once, P4[6:8:10].

16th row As 4th row.

17th row P4[6:8:10], * K5, P5, Cr3L, P1,
Cr3R, P5, K5 *, P2, K8, P2, rep from * to
* once, P4[6:8:10].

18th row As 2nd row.

These 18 rows form the patt. Cont in
patt until 2nd[12th:2nd:14th] row of
5th[5th:6th:6th] patt has been worked.

Shape shoulders

Bind off 9 sts at beg of next 4 rows and
7[8:9:10] sts at beg of foll 2 rows.
Bind off.

Left front

Using No. 6 (4½mm) needles cast on
19 sts for pocket lining. Beg with a P row,
work 21 rows reverse stockinette st, inc
one st at each end of last row. Cut off yarn
and leave these 21 sts on a holder.

Using No. 3 (3¼mm) needles cast on
29[31:33:35] sts. Work 18 rows ribbing
as given for back.

Next row Rib to end, inc 7 sts evenly
across the row. 36[38:40:42] sts.
Change to No. 6 (4½mm) needles.

Next row P1, K1, P1, K2, P5, (K6, P5)
twice, K4[6:8:10].

Begin patt.

1st row (RS) P4[6:8:10], rep from * to
* of 1st row of back, P2, K1, P1, K1.

2nd row P1, K1, P1, K2, rep from * to

of 2nd row of back, K4[6:8:10].

3rd row P4[6:8:10], rep from * to * of
3rd row of back, P2, K1, P1, K1.

4th row P1, K1, K2, rep from * to * of
4th row of back, K4[6:8:10].

Keeping 3 sts in rib at front edge, cont in
patt as now set until 2nd row of 2nd patt
has been completed.

Divide for pocket

Next row Patt 7[9:11:13], bind off
next 21 sts in patt, patt to end.

Next row Patt 8, K the sts of pocket
lining, patt to end. 36[38:40:42] sts.
Cont in patt until 13th[1st:9th:1st] row
of 4th[5th:5th:6th] patt has been
worked.

Shape neck

Next row Bind off 6 sts, patt to end.
Keeping patt correct, dec one st at neck
edge on every row to 26[30:30:32]
sts, then on every other row until 25
[26:27:28] sts rem.

Shape shoulder

Bind off 9 sts at beg of next and foll
alternate row. Work 1 row. Bind off.

Right front

Work to match left front, reversing
shaping and position patt as foll:

1st row K1, P1, K1, P2, rep from * to
* of 1st row of back, P4[6:8:10].

Left sleeve

Using No. 6 (4½mm) needles cast on
19 sts for pocket lining. Beg with a P row,
work 21 rows reverse stockinette st,
ending with a P row.

Cut off yarn and leave sts on a holder.

Using No. 3 (3¼mm) needles cast on
35[37:39:41] sts. Work 2½[2½:3:3]in
(6.5[6.5:7.5:7.5]cm) ribbing as given for
back, ending with a 2nd row. Change to
No. 6 (4½mm) needles. Beg with a P row,
cont in reverse stockinette st, inc one st
each end of 5th and every foll 6th row to
47[53:57:63] sts. Work 3[1:3:1] rows
straight.

Divide for pocket

Next row P14[17:19:22], bind off next
19 sts, P to end.

Next row K14[17:19:22], K sts of pocket
lining, K to end. 47[53:57:63] sts.
Cont to inc one st each end of every 6th
row until there are 51[55:61:65] sts.
Work 1[5:1:5] rows straight, ending

102

with a K row. Rib 7 rows. Bind off in ribbing.

Right sleeve
Work as for left sleeve, omitting pocket.

Neckband
Join shoulder seams. With RS of work facing, join yarn to right front neck and using No. 3 (3¼mm) needles, pick up 18[20:21:23] sts from right front neck, 24[26:28:30] sts from back neck and 19[21:22:24] sts from left front neck. 61[67:71:77] sts. Beg with a 2nd row, rib 16 rows. Bind off loosely in ribbing.

To finish
Press or block according to directions on yarn wrapper. Sew zippers into pocket openings, then sew down pocket linings. Mark depth of armholes 5[5½:6:6½]in (12.5[14:15:16.5]cm) from shoulder seams on back and fronts. Sew sleeves to armholes between markers, then join side and sleeve seams. Sew in zipper. Fold neckband to wrong side; slip stitch in position. Press seams.

Jacket with collar
Back and fronts
Work as for jacket with neckband, omitting pockets on fronts.

Sleeves
Work as for sleeves of jacket with neckband, omitting pocket.

Collar
Using No. 3 (3¼mm) needles cast on 79 [85:91:97] sts.
1st row K1, (P1, K1) to end.
2nd row P1, (K1, P1) to end.
Rep these 2 rows for 7 [8:8:9]cm. Bind off in ribbing.

To finish
Press or block according to yarn used. Mark depth of armholes 5[5½:6:6½]in (12.5[14:15:16.5]cm) from shoulder seams on back and fronts. Sew sleeves to armholes between markers, then join side and sleeve seams. Sew cast-on edge of collar to neck. Sew in zipper. Press seams.

Technique tip
How to make Aran "bobbles"

Bobbles are a feature of many traditional Aran patterns: they are the "rocks" or "boulders" in the "seascapes" represented in textured panels of knitting.

In this pattern, reverse stockinette stitch is used to make the bobbles even more distinct against a stockinette stitch background. The precise directions for making a bobble are always found in the pattern, but it is useful to understand the general principles. The idea is to increase to five stitches from one, work on these separately, then decrease to the original single stitch.

remaining loop in the usual way: there is now the original stitch plus four extra on the right-hand needle.

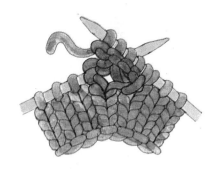

Continue working on these five stitches to form the bobble. Turn the work and knit five stitches, then turn again and purl them.

When you reach the position for a bobble, knit the next stitch without letting it slide off the left-hand needle. Bring the yarn forward and knit the loop remaining on the left-hand needle.

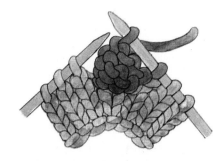

To shape the bobbles, decrease over the center 3 stitches of the bobble on the next row as follows: slip 1, K2 together, pass the slipped stitch over. On the following row knit together the 3 remaining stitches of the bobble to complete it. The right side of the knitting is facing you: continue knitting the pattern from the point where you broke off.

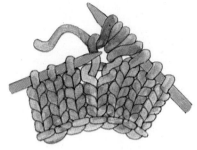

Again, don't allow the loop to slide off the left-hand needle. Bring the yarn forward and over again and knit into the

Soft look. . . .

What could be easier to make or more stunning than this pretty overblouse? The soft cotton version is trimmed with lace edging. It looks good with jeans, shorts or a skirt. For colder days, the same design can be made in tweed as an open-sided tunic trimmed with braid.

Measurements
To fit sizes 10–18.
Finished length 27½in (70cm).

Materials
1¾yd (1.5m) of 54in (104cm)-wide lightweight cotton
2⅜yd (2.1m) of ¾in (2cm)-wide lace edging
1⅛yd (1m) of 1½in (4cm)-wide seam binding or ribbon in matching shade
Matching thread, tailor's chalk

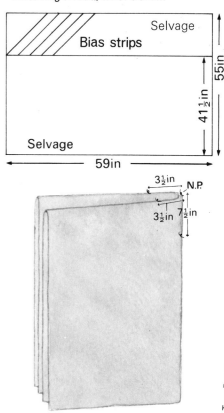

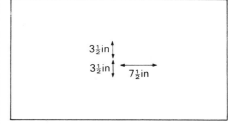

Terry Evans

1 Cut fabric into rectangle, 41½ x 59in (105 x 150cm). Fold in half across width and then lengthwise. With tailor's tack mark top right-hand corner, where folds intersect. This is center neck point (NP). For neck opening, measure and mark 3½in (9cm) each side of neck point and 7½in (19cm) down center front.

2 Open fabric out. Draw lines between tacks, using tailor's chalk, and cut along them to form neck and center front opening.

Caroline Arber

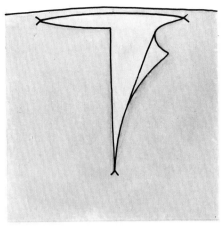

3 Make $\frac{1}{8}$in (3mm) cuts at ends of neck and bottom of center front opening.

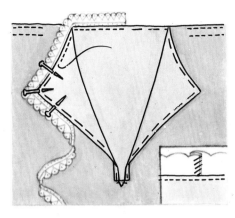

5 Starting at center back, pin, baste and stitch lace all around collar and front opening. Overlap and finish lace by hand at center back.

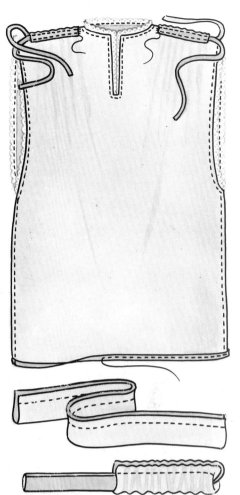

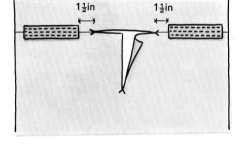

4 Cut two 14$\frac{1}{2}$in (37cm) lengths of binding or ribbon for casings. Turn in $\frac{3}{8}$in (1cm) at each end of binding to finish. Position binding along one shoulder line. End of binding should be 1$\frac{1}{2}$in (4cm) from neck opening. Pin and baste in place. Work a line of machine stitching down center of binding and two more lines $\frac{5}{8}$in (15mm) on each side of center. Repeat to make second casing.

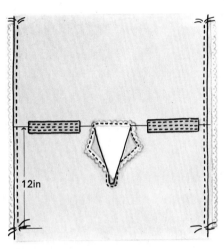

6 To establish underarm points, measure 12in (30cm) down each side of shoulder lines. Starting at underarm point, stitch lace all around each armhole, finishing ends. Stitch sides of overshirt using French seams.

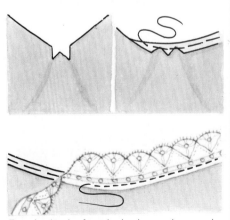

7 Cut four bias strips of fabric for drawstrings, each 1$\frac{1}{2}$in x 15$\frac{3}{4}$in (4 x 40cm). Make drawstrings and thread through shoulder casings, tacking at inner ends of casings. Pull up ties to gather shoulders. Turn under and make a narrow machine-stitched hem at lower edge.

Technique tips Attaching lace and braid

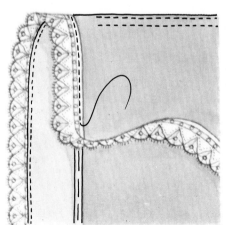

The basic method for attaching: turn over a $\frac{1}{8}$in (3mm) hem to right side of fabric and press. Pin the lace or braid over the raw edge, baste and machine stitch.

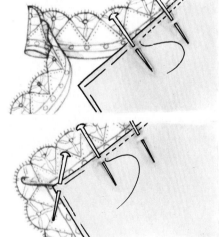

To turn a corner, as on the collar point, fold the lace or braid, as illustrated, to make a right angled corner.

For the end of a slashed opening, make $\frac{1}{8}$in (3mm) slashes at the end of the opening. Open out the slash to lie flat. Apply lace or braid, easing it around the slashes — it will stand up a little when collar is closed, but lie flat when open.

Terry Evans

105

. . . Sporty look

Neil Kirk

Materials

54in (140cm)-wide tweed:
For the length shown here (approx 29½in [75cm] from back of neck to hem) buy 7⅞yd (80cm) of fabric. To lengthen, add 2in (5cm) to length you want from neck to hem; this gives you the quantity to buy
7⅛yd (6.5m) of narrow braid for binding and ties
1⅛yd (1m) of 1½in (4cm)-wide seam binding or ribbon in matching shade
Matching thread, tailor's chalk

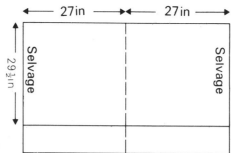

1 Cut fabric to create a piece that measures the width of the fabric by the back length (29½in [75cm] if you are making the length shown here), then cut in half across width as diagram. Mark neck and front opening on one piece using the measurements given on page 104.

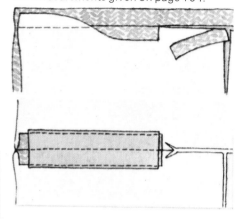

2 Lay the two pieces together with right sides facing, making ⅝in (1.5cm) seams, pin, baste and stitch shoulder seams. Press seams open. Using seam binding or ribbon, make casings for ties as shown on page 105. Trim seam allowance from neck edge.

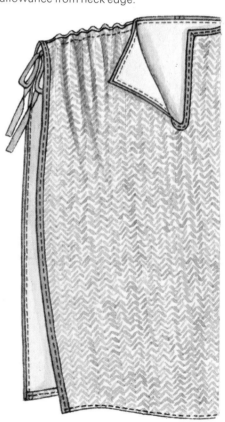

3 Starting at center back, attach braid all around collar and front opening. Turn ends of braid under and overcast neatly at center back.
4 Stitch braid down both side edges, turn ends under to finish. Cut remainder of braid into four equal pieces for ties. Thread through casings, securing as in Step 7.
Hem by machine as for cotton version.

EXTRA SPECIAL SEWING

Pretty and practical pinafore

Two simple decorative ideas give an original look to these pleated pinafores. A young girl can wear one with a dress for a pretty party look, or over pants and top for everyday.

George Wright

Measurements

These directions are for sizes: 5/6 and 7/8 (chest $22\frac{7}{8}$ and 26in) (58 and 66cm). The pattern allows $\frac{3}{8}$in (1cm) for seams and hems on armhole and $\frac{3}{4}$in (2cm) for bottom hem.

Materials

Size 5/6: 1yd (.9m) of 36in (90cm)-wide fabric, $\frac{7}{8}$yd (.8m) of 48in (122cm)-wide fabric
Size 7/8: $1\frac{1}{8}$yd (1m) of 36in (90cm)-wide fabric, $\frac{7}{8}$yd (.8m) of 48in (122cm)-wide fabric
Suggested fabrics: lightweight denim, corduroy, cottons
3 ball buttons; thread
1 skein tapestry yarn for cross-stitching or $\frac{5}{8}$yd (.5m) of $\frac{1}{4}$in (6mm)-wide satin ribbon and 5 beads for trim

1 Measure and cut out garment pieces. Mark positions of shoulder straps on dress back pieces.

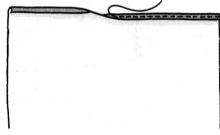

2 On top edge of center front panel turn over small hem and machine stitch. Press.

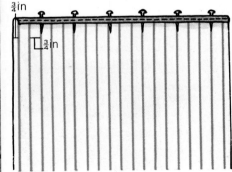

3 Measure the panel for pleats, leaving $\frac{3}{4}$in (2cm) at each end. On wrong side, mark positions for six $\frac{3}{4}$in (2cm) pleats, using chalk. Pins mark fold lines.

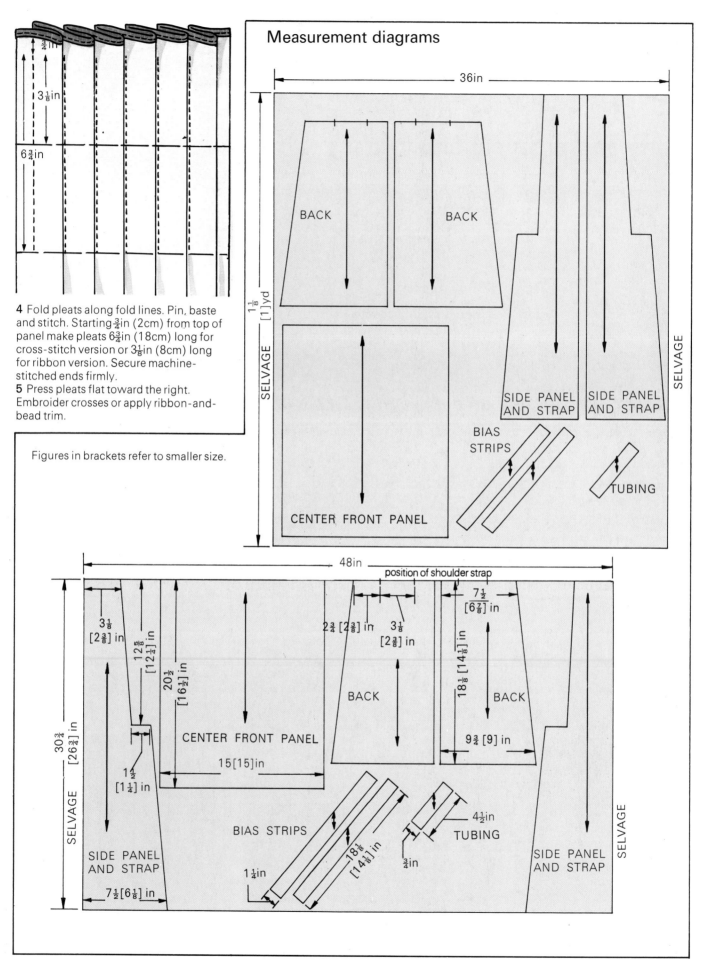

4 Fold pleats along fold lines. Pin, baste and stitch. Starting $\frac{3}{4}$in (2cm) from top of panel make pleats $6\frac{3}{4}$in (18cm) long for cross-stitch version or $3\frac{1}{8}$in (8cm) long for ribbon version. Secure machine-stitched ends firmly.

5 Press pleats flat toward the right. Embroider crosses or apply ribbon-and-bead trim.

Figures in brackets refer to smaller size.

$\frac{3}{4}$in

$3\frac{1}{8}$in

$6\frac{3}{4}$in

Measurement diagrams

36in

$1\frac{1}{8}$ [1]yd

SELVAGE

SELVAGE

BACK

BACK

SIDE PANEL AND STRAP

SIDE PANEL AND STRAP

BIAS STRIPS

TUBING

CENTER FRONT PANEL

48in

position of shoulder strap

SELVAGE

SELVAGE

$3\frac{1}{8}$ [$2\frac{3}{8}$] in

$12\frac{5}{8}$ [$12\frac{1}{4}$] in

$20\frac{1}{2}$ [$16\frac{1}{2}$] in

$30\frac{3}{4}$ [$26\frac{3}{4}$] in

$1\frac{1}{2}$ [$1\frac{1}{4}$] in

CENTER FRONT PANEL

15[15]in

$2\frac{3}{4}$ [$2\frac{3}{8}$] in $3\frac{1}{8}$ [$2\frac{3}{8}$] in

$7\frac{1}{2}$ [$6\frac{7}{8}$] in

$18\frac{1}{8}$ [$14\frac{1}{8}$] in

BACK

BACK

$9\frac{3}{4}$ [9] in

BIAS STRIPS

$18\frac{1}{8}$ [$14\frac{1}{8}$] in

TUBING

$4\frac{1}{2}$in

$\frac{3}{4}$in

$1\frac{1}{4}$in

SIDE PANEL AND STRAP

$7\frac{1}{2}$[$6\frac{1}{8}$] in

SIDE PANEL AND STRAP

6 With right sides together pin and baste side panels to pleated center front panel. Machine stitch. Press seams together toward sides of garment. Finish raw edges.

7 With right sides together pin and baste dress backs to side fronts, keeping fabric grain straight at center back. Machine stitch. Press seams open. Finish.

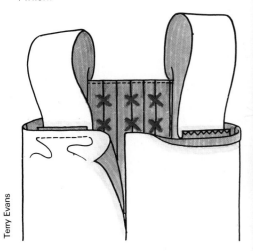

8 Position shoulder straps on dress backs, right sides together, pin, baste and machine stitch. Press seams open. Finish.

Terry Evans

Steve Bicknell

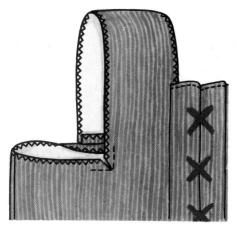

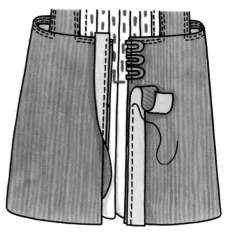

9 Reinforce the corners at front armholes with machine stitching. Snip ⅜in (1cm) through seam allowances at corners. Finish raw edges.

10 Turn hem allowance to wrong side at neck edge and armholes. Sew two lines of topstitching on the right side.

11 For button loops—make three strips of tubing 1½in (4cm) long. Pin loops to right half of center back. With right sides together pin and baste bias strip to both center back edges and stitch as close to the edge as possible. (On the right-hand side you will be stitching through loops, strip and dress.)

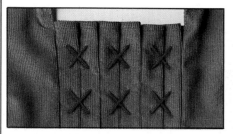

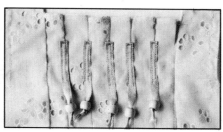

Technique tip

Decorating the center front panels

12 Turn bias strips to the wrong side and press. Turn raw edge of bias strip under ⅛in (3mm), baste and press. On the right side stitch two lines of topstitching down entire length of both center back edges.

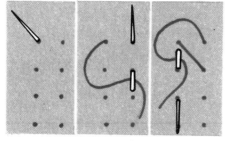

1 For cross-stitch version mark the positions of the crosses starting at the top left-hand pleat, ¾in (2cm) from the top of the panel. Each cross is ¾in (2cm) across and ¾in (2cm) down and there is a ¾in (2cm) space between each cross. Mark four crosses on every other pleat, using tailor's tacks or tailor's chalk.

3 For ribbon version, cut five pieces of ribbon 4in (10cm) long and thread a bead on each one. Knot each ribbon at end to hold beads on. Trim ribbons to the same length, cutting ends diagonally to prevent fraying. Pin in position over each pleat, ¾in (2cm) from the top of the center panel. Topstitch ribbons in place, tucking raw ends in to finish and stitching 1½in (4cm) down each side.

2 To sew the stitches, use a darning needle and a single strand of yarn and start at the top left-hand corner of each pleat, securing with a firm knot before you start. When you reach the bottom of the pleat, finish with a firm knot and start again at the top of the next pleat.

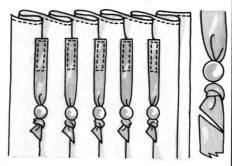

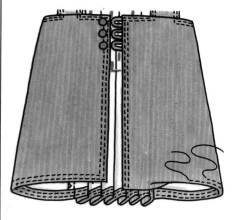

13 Sew ball buttons to left side. Turn up a ¾in (2cm) hem. Baste. Secure with two rows of topstitching.

SEWING

Sweet-dreaming nightgown

Set aside just a few hours and make yourself a pretty one-size nightie. Very adaptable — it can be made in whatever fabric you like. We've made it in a pretty printed cotton and in a double-layered version for a really glamorous look.

John Carter

111

Size

The directions given here will make a gown to fit any size from bust 31½in (80cm) upward. The smaller you are, the fuller the gathers, but there is sufficient material in the nightgown to fit larger figures very comfortably.

Materials

3⅛yd (2.8m) of 36in (90cm) or 45in (115cm)-wide lawn or batiste or 3⅙yd (2.8m) each of chiffon and a lightweight satin-like fabric for the layered version.

2¼yd (2m) of 2in (5cm)-wide eyelet embroidery or lace trim (lace is best for the two-layered version)

4yd (3.6m) of ⅜in (1cm)-wide seam binding for casing.

2¼yd (2m) of elastic cord: allow more for larger sizes

Matching sewing thread (silk thread is best for chiffon and fine fabrics)

Note the cutting method is the same for both fabric widths.

single strip 1½ x 36in (4 x 90cm)

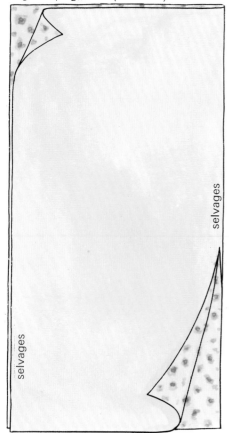

1 Trim the fabric so that it is even at both ends. For the shoulder straps cut a 1½in (4cm) wide strip from one end of the fabric. Fold the remainder of the fabric lengthwise with two cut edges together and cut along the foldline.

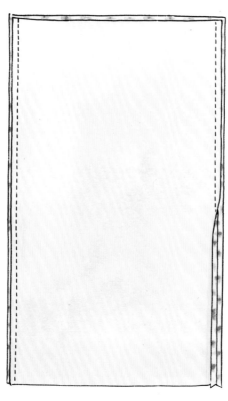

2 Baste the two pieces of fabric together, right sides facing, along the long selvage edges. Leave a seam allowance of about ⅝ (1.5cm). Stitch these side seams. Remove basting and press the seams open.

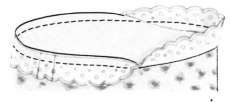

3 Pin the trimming to the top of the nightgown, right sides facing, beginning at one side seam. Make a narrow seam in the trimming to match the side seam. Finish the raw edges of this seam in the trimming by hand or machine overcasting. Baste and stitch the trimming to the top of the nightgown. Press the seam down and carefully trim to ¼in (6mm).

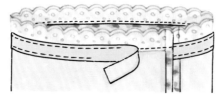

4 Cut two lengths of seam binding to fit around the top of the nightgown, plus ⅜in (1cm) to turn under at each end. Beginning at one side seam, pin one length of ribbon to the wrong side

of the nightgown top, just below the row of machine stitching, and turn under the raw ends where they meet.

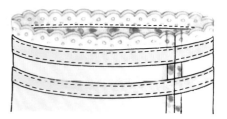

Stitch close to the edge of each side of the ribbon. Stitch the second row of ribbon below the first in the same way, leaving a 1¼in (3cm) gap between them.

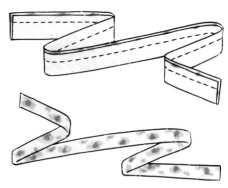

5 To make the shoulder straps, cut two 18in (45.5cm) lengths from the 1½in (4cm)-wide strip. Fold each strap in half lengthwise, right sides together. Baste and stitch ⅜in (1cm) away from the folded edge.

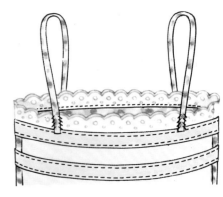

6 Turn the straps right side out. Baste close to stitched edge and press flat. Finish the raw edges at each end by overcasting by hand. Catch stitch the straps into position on the wrong side of the nightgown, then catch stitch the trimming to the straps.

Opposite page: Creamy lace adds luxury to the two-layered nightgown. Ribbon could be used for straps.

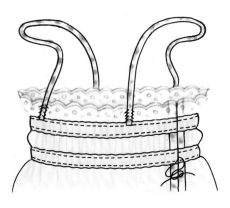

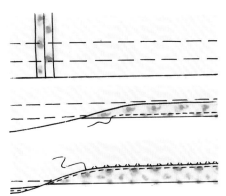

7 Cut the elastic cord into two lengths. Using a bodkin, thread one length of elastic through each casing tape. Draw up the elastic to fit comfortably and secure the ends firmly in a figure eight knot. Trim off the excess elastic.

8 Try on the night gown and mark the hem length plus ½in (1.3cm) hem allowance. Fold up along the ½in (1.3cm) line and baste close to the folded edge. Machine stitch close to the folded edge and trim away excess fabric close to the stitching. Turn up along the hemline and sew the hem up by hand.

The directions are the same for both the cotton version and the layered version, but make sure that you note the following points when making the layered one.

Technique tip

Working a hand-rolled hem

For fabrics that are delicate, fine or slippery, a hand-rolled hem is the best way to get a neat, lightweight finish.
Make a line of machine stitching ⅛in (3mm) below the marked line for the hem. Trim, so that the stitching is about ⅛in (3mm) from the raw edge.
Fold the hem to the wrong side along a line just above the stitching. Press, evenly

and very carefully.
Using a fine needle, working from right to left, make a stitch through the fold, then a stitch in the nightgown. The stitch should be diagonal and pick up just a single strand. Make about six stitches, about ⅛in (3mm) apart, then pull up the thread in order to draw down the fold and make a neat, rolled hem.

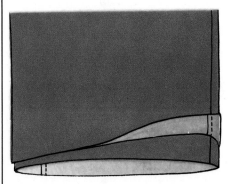

1 When cutting out your fabrics, cut out both identically.

2 Join the side seams on both layers, using the French seam method, and put the satin layer inside the chiffon layer, wrong sides of both facing body.

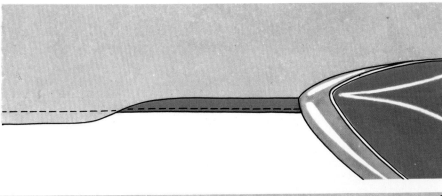

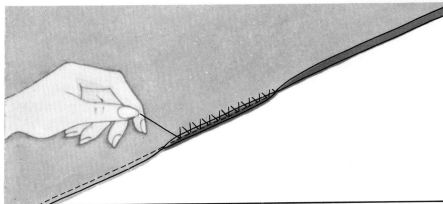

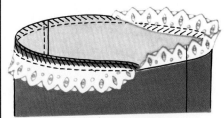

3 Before applying lace, be sure to match side seams of both layers. Finish all three raw edges (including lace trim) together with hand overcasting.

4 Work hand-rolled hems. The two hems must be worked on the wrong sides of both layers.

Homemaker

Drapery and curtain know-how (1)

Make your own curtains and draperies with our help. We start with a check list of points to consider in choosing styles and a guide to calculating the correct amount of fabric

Making your own curtains and draperies is one of the biggest money-savers in home sewing. All the do-it-yourself curtain accessories on the market today make it a fairly simple job, giving you the freedom of choice in style and fabric to achieve a professional, individual look to suit every room in the house.

Choosing the style and fabric — Before buying any fabric or sewing your first stitch, consider the style, length and color of curtains or draperies that will best suit your windows and complement the room. In part, this is a question of personal taste and the style of your furnishings. If you have a modern home with contemporary furniture, ornate brocades and rich damasks would probably look out of place; consider a modern-style fabric. If you want to achieve a period look,

consider a fabric that reflects the right period flavor. Besides the "style" of your home and furnishings, there are some basic design points to consider:

Size of room — generally large designs and bold colors look best in a large room. But remember that too much pattern can be tiresome, so it is importance to achieve the correct balance between the size of the room and the pattern used. Small designs and soft colors are best for small rooms.

Kind of room — consider what the room is used for and whether you spend a lot of time in it. For rooms that take heavy wear, such as bathrooms and kitchens, curtains should be made in a casual style and a practical fabric that is steam-resistant and will wash and wear

well. For less heavily used rooms, such as living rooms, dining rooms or bedrooms, the draperies could be made in a more luxurious fabric and elegant style.

Size and shape of windows — windows come in all shapes and sizes, some are tall and narrow, some short and wide and some are arranged in uneven groups. Use curtains or draperies to their best advantage, so they disguise rather than accentuate window problems. Draperies may cover an entire wall if necessary.

There are basically three lengths to choose from — sill length, below the sill or floor length. Sill-length draperies or curtains should just clear the sill and floor length ones should end about 1 in (2.5cm) from the floor to prevent unnecessary wear.

Tie-back curtains cover window frame.

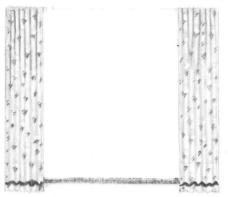

Extended rod gives extra width.

An elegant look with draperies extended to the floor.

A fabric-covered cornice board creates a smaller window area.

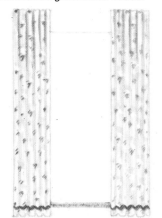

Rod fixed above the window gives extra height.

It's often difficult to visualize the optical effects different styles will create. These illustrations should help you — all the ideas are applied to the same size window.

Terry Evans

Measuring your windows and calculating the fabric

1 Decide on the length of draperies or curtains you want and the placement of the rod and measure, using our diagram as a guide. Measure from the top of a conventional rod and from the bottom of the rings on a decorative rod. Add extra length for hem and heading according to the style you want. For draperies made with pleater tape, allow $\frac{1}{2}$in (13mm) at the top for attaching tape and 8in (20cm) for a double hem at the bottom.

2 Measure the width of your rod and add $1\frac{1}{2}$in (4cm) for side hems plus the width of return to the wall and overlap at the center. For a pinch-pleated heading you should double the width to provide fullness.

3 Divide the width measurement by the width of the fabric you are buying to give you the number of fabric widths you will need, allowing an additional $1\frac{1}{4}$in (3cm) for each seam needed. Always count a fraction as a full width.

4 Multiply the length measurement by this total. This will give you the amount of fabric required.

Note If your fabric is not pre-shrunk, add approximately $1\frac{1}{4}$in per yard (3cm per meter) for shrinkage to the overall fabric requirements.

Pattern-matching

If the fabric you have chosen has a pattern that repeats itself, the patterns will have to be matched so that they run at the same level on all the panels. This means buying extra fabric. Measure the pattern repeat and allow for one pattern repeat per width after the first, i.e., if three widths of material are needed for the window, purchase extra material for pattern repeats.

Buying fabrics

When buying fabrics, always head straight for the furnishing department. As attractive as the designs or price of dress fabrics may be, they lack the body and special qualities such as resistance to sunlight found in furnishing fabrics.

Informal fabrics suitable for curtains or draperies include chintz, polished cotton, gingham and linen. More formal fabrics include velvet, brocade and damask.

A polished cotton
B ribbed cotton
C damask
D chintz
E homespun
F brocade
G gingham
H velvet

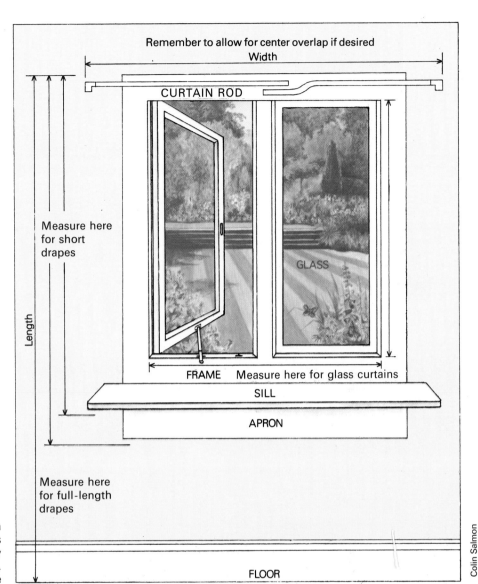

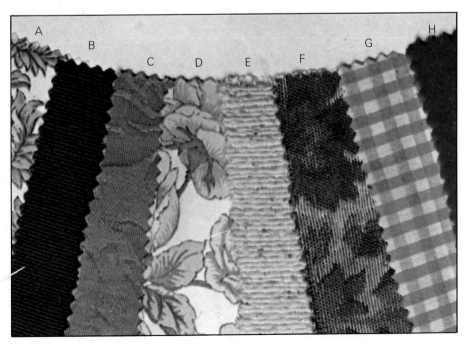

Colin Salmon

Lining

Draperies and curtains may be lined to improve the hang, insulation and lengthen the life of the fabric by protecting it from dirt, sunlight and pollution. Check that the lining fabric is pre-shrunk to avoid uneven shrinkage of the fabric and lining in laundering. The same rules apply to buying lining fabric as to the drapery fabric. Do not try to economize by buying inexpensive material that may spoil the finished effect. Choose a suitable lining to match the curtain fabric. Cotton sateen in a neutral color such as white, light beige or soft grey is often chosen.

Accessories

A wide range of rods for curtains and draperies is available and can provide a variety of professional looks. Traverse rods come in a plain style designed to be covered by the drapery heading and in a number of decorative designs which remain visible above the top edge of the draperies. Traverse rods are also available with two tracks — one for a valance on the outside and one for the draperies inside or one for the draperies outside and one for glass curtains inside. Most traverse rods can be attached to wall, ceiling or window frame. They can be expanded in length and in distance from the wall or window frame.

Weights

Draperies and curtains can also be given a professional look by the use of weights to make them hang properly. Weights can be purchased individually or in the form of lead-weighted chains. The chain is best for lightweight fabrics. Simply insert it along the bottom hem and tack securely at each end. For heavier fabrics, tack individual weights to the bottom corners and to the seams of each panel.

Headings

Curtain and drapery-making has been greatly simplified by the introduction of pleater tape that can be used with special hooks to make pinch-pleated headings. The tape can be used to produce a heading that covers the rod and eliminates the need for a valance or one for use with rings and a decorative rod. Pleater tape can also be used to make cafe curtains with a scalloped edge along the top. Clip-on and sew-on hooks are also available to make scalloped, pleated or tubular headings on cafe curtains.

The simple yet elegant look of pinch-pleated draperies is particularly well suited to modern furnishings.

Elizabeth Whiting

Homemaker

Drapery and curtain know-how (2)

Really professional, lined draperies that hang beautifully are among the most important features in a living room or bedroom. This second chapter on drapery and curtain know-how gives you the step-by-step method for making classic fully-lined draperies using pleater tape for the heading.

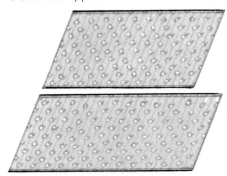

First measure your windows and determine your fabric requirements following the method given in the previous Homemaker chapter, "Drapery and Curtain Know-How (1)." You will need drapery fabric, lining fabric, pleater tape and matching sewing thread.

Cutting out
Press fabric to remove all creases and carefully examine for any flaws. Lay the fabric on a large flat surface and straighten the edges. To do this mark a line at right angles to the selvage (if possible, draw a thread as a guideline). On full-length draperies try to get an unbroken pattern repeat at the top, since the hem will be less noticeable. On short-length draperies the reverse applies.

1 Cut the first length, then, if using a patterned fabric, cut all further lengths using this first length as a guideline to ensure patterns match at the seams. Press and cut out the lining to the same measurements as the drapery pieces.

Joining the lengths of fabric

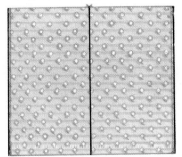

1 Making sure that all fabric patterns run in the same direction, pin together, taking $1\frac{1}{4}$ to $1\frac{1}{2}$in (3 to 3.5cm) seams. Stitch, using a fairly long stitch.

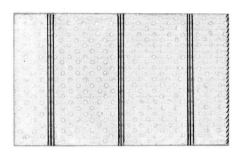

2 If you are making a pair of drapery panels with an uneven number of fabric widths, one width will have to be cut in half lengthwise. Join this fabric width, using the selvage to make the seam and the raw edge the side hem. The wider fabric widths should be placed toward the center of the window, the half widths at the sides. Overcast raw edges. Press.

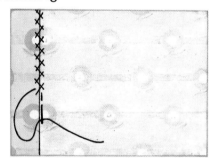

3 To release any tension in the fabric, the selvage should be snipped at approximately 4in (10cm) intervals throughout. Join lining pieces in the same way. Press.

Hemming

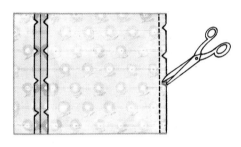

1 Turn under a 1½in (4cm) hem at sides of each drapery panel, baste and press. Catch stitch invisibly to panel.

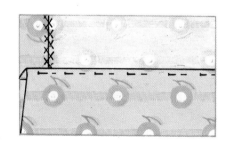

2 For the bottom hem, turn under ½in (1.3cm) and press. Turn under a further 4in (10cm), pin and press.

3 Where the bottom and side hems meet, there will be an extra thickness of material, which should be removed by mitering to give a flat hem. Miter the hem at each corner as follows:

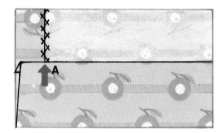

a At point A on bottom hem mark intersection with side hem.

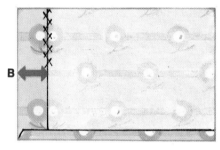

b Open out bottom hem and cut into side hem to point B along fold line.

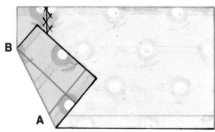

c Fold hem from point B to A.

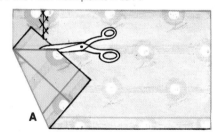

d Fold bottom hem back into position and note unnecessary triangle at B. Cut away.

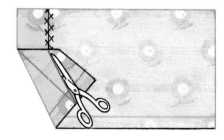

e Trim side hem allowance to 1½in (4cm) as shown.

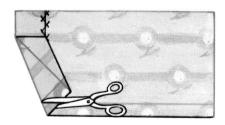

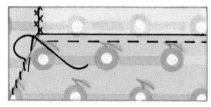

f Turn under the first turning of the hem and another small triangle is formed. Snip away.

g Fold hem back into position and baste. Slip stitch hem to panel, being careful that no stitches show on the right side. Slip stitch mitered corners to side hems.

4 Turn under ½in (1.3cm) hem at the bottom edge of the lining. Press. Turn under another 5in (12.5cm). Slip stitch in place. Do not miter corners or make side hems in the lining at this stage.

Locking in the lining

1 A lining is locked to thick fabrics to prevent it from falling away from the top fabric when the draperies are hanging. Locking is usually worked at 12in (30cm) intervals across a drapery panel and should begin and end 8in (20cm) from both bottom and top.

a Place the panel on a flat surface with wrong side on top. Lay the lining on the panel, wrong sides together, placing the hem edge of the lining 1 to 2in (2.5 to 5cm) above the panel hem edge. On each single-width panel 48in (122cm) wide, make three rows of locking, one down the middle of the panel and one on each side, 12in (30cm) in from the edge.

Marion Appleton

3 Pin, baste and stitch along the sides and lower edge of the tape making sure to leave pocket openings free. On some kinds of tape the stitching guideline is actually woven into the tape.

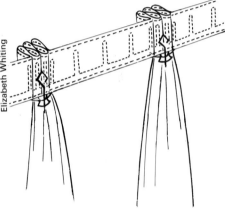

Elizabeth Whiting

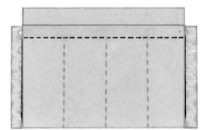

b Work loop stitch as follows: fold back the lining along the center; join the thread to hem. Spacing stitches about 2in (5cm) apart, pick up one thread of lining fabric and one of panel, having thread under needle to form a loop stitch. Complete the other two rows, one on each side of the center row.

Attaching a pleater tape heading

1 Cut pleater tape 1in (2.5cm) longer than the drapery panel and place pocket side up on the right side of the panel with pocket openings at the top.

The bottom of the tape should cover the upper edge of the panel by $\frac{1}{2}$in (1.3cm) and the ends of the tape should extend $\frac{1}{2}$in (1.3cm) beyond each side of the panel. Pin, baste and stitch the tape to the panel and lining along the bottom edge of the tape.

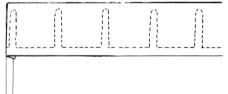

2 When the locking is completed, lay the lining flat again, turn in the side edges and pin to the panel so that $\frac{3}{4}$in (2cm) of panel is showing. Slip stitch lining to panel on both sides. Make a line of basting stitches 1in (2.5cm) from the top to hold the lining firmly in place until the pleater tape is attached. Trim away any extra fabric above the panel.

2 Fold the tape down over the lining on the wrong side of the panel and tuck the seam allowance under at the sides.

4 Pleat panel by inserting the four prongs of the pleater hooks into four consecutive pockets. Skip three pockets between hooks. Use single-prong hooks at center front where panels overlap when closed and on returns. To insure neat folds in the finished draperies, hang, pull open and tie a piece of cotton tape or string loosely around each panel arranging pleats carefully. Pin tape in place with T-pins. You may also pin the pleats in place at the bottom. Remove pins and tape after a few days.

Other styles of heading

For more flexibility in spacing pinch pleats or for different types of pleats such as cartridge, box, or French pleats, stiffen the headings of each panel with a backing such as buckram and make the pleats by measuring and stitching them individually. In order to apply stiffening to the headings it is advisable to use the same method as for pleater tape.

Pinch-pleated draperies can be tied back in the daytime to let in light and closed at night to provide privacy and muffle street noise (see above).

Homemaker

Patchwork quilt cover

This easy-to-make quilt cover is a lovely way to introduce a touch of individuality into your bedroom.

For the patches, you can use up remnants or have fun choosing a selection of new fabrics. The back of the cover is made from a double sheet.

Materials
One flat double sheet
49 squares of fabric, each 11 in (28cm) square
60 triangles of fabric, with shorter edges measuring 9in (23cm) and the long edge measuring 13in (33cm)
All fabrics should be colorfast, washable, and of the same weight
To make version in photograph, buy 1⅝yd (1.4m) of print fabric in center patch; 1⅜yd (1.2m) each of two other prints and one solid fabric
2¼yd (2m) seam binding
2⅜yd (2.1m) of 1 in (2.5cm)-wide bias binding; matching thread

The cover measures 78¾ x 78¾in (200 x 200cm) and will fit a double-size continental quilt. Seam allowance is ⅝in (1.5cm) unless otherwise stated.

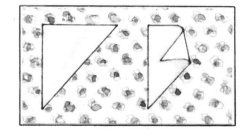

2 Cut out your squares and triangles. When cutting the triangles, make sure one edge of each triangle is along the straight grain (weave) of the fabric. Make a paper pattern for the triangle to help you cut accurately.

3 Finish the edges of each square and triangle by zig-zag stitching by machine or overcasting by hand.

Terry Evans

1 Start by planning the patchwork. Draw the pattern of squares and triangles shown in the diagram on a piece of paper. Use this to plan which patches are to be in each of your available fabrics, to get the best combination of colors and patterns. You can work out at this stage whether you have enough fabric or how much you need to buy. Once you have bought or selected the fabrics, wash them before cutting out to avoid the risk of uneven shrinkage.

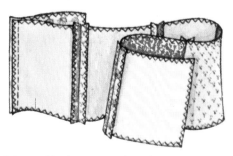

4 Assemble the squares into the pattern selected. With right sides together, sew the squares into seven strips. Press seams open.

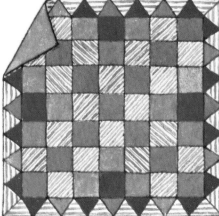

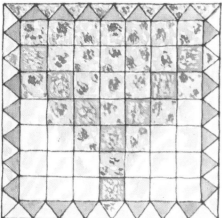

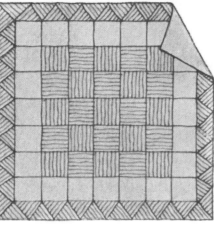

You can reproduce this effective patchwork in any color scheme. Choose one solid-color fabric and three small-print patterned fabrics in a similar color.

Three alternative ideas for the patchwork scheme, showing different combinations of solid and print fabrics.

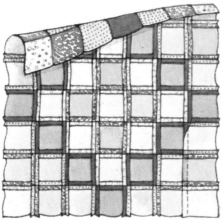

5 Matching seamlines, with right sides together, stitch the seven strips together. Press seams open.

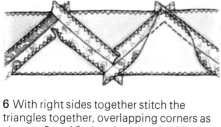

6 With right sides together stitch the triangles together, overlapping corners as shown. Sew 15 triangles in each of four strips. Press.

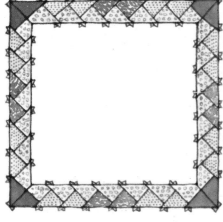

7 With right sides together join the four strips at each corner to form a square. Press.

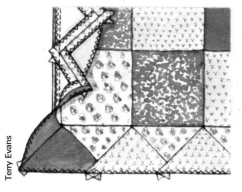

8 Stitch the outer square to the center square section, right sides together,

matching seamlines. Trim and overcast the edges. Press the seams open.

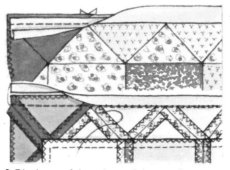

9 Bind one of the edges of the patchwork with bias binding —this is now the bottom edge.

10 Cut sheet to measure 80in (203cm) x 90$\frac{3}{8}$in (230cm). Finish the edges by machine zig-zag or hand overcasting.

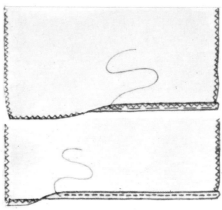

11 Fold up $\frac{3}{4}$in (2cm) along one of the shorter edges and baste or pin, then fold up another $\frac{3}{4}$in (2cm) and stitch to make a double hem. This is now the bottom edge.

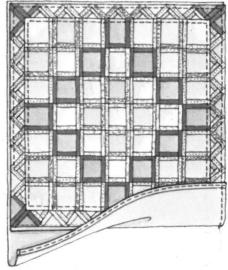

12 Place patchwork and sheet together with right sides facing and even at the top edge. Fold bottom 8$\frac{1}{4}$in (21cm) of sheet over wrong side of patchwork to form flap. Baste and stitch down sides and along top of cover.

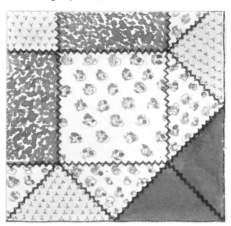

13 Turn right side out and press. You can outline the patchwork with zig-zag stitch on the right side if you wish.

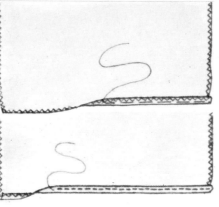

14 Cut the seam binding into eight equal pieces. Sew four pieces at regular intervals 1 in (2.5cm) inside the flap edge, and match the other four inside the patchwork edge. These tapes tie together to hold the quilt securely inside.

Terry Evans

Homemaker

Trim your towels

Towels are always a welcome present and you can make them special by decorating them with appliqué. These graceful motifs could also brighten up old towels you have in your linen closet. The appliqué is quickly and easily done by machine. Or you can hand-embroider the motifs for a more traditional look.

Materials
  Set of 4 towels—we used 2 guest
    towels and 2 hand towels in 2
    complementary shades of green
    (but any size will do)
  Small amount of light and dark green
    satin
  Small amount of floral print cotton
    fabric
  Matching light and dark green sewing
    thread
  Tracing paper
  Small amount of thin cardboard to
    make pattern
  Soft pencil
  Tailor's chalk

Clive Helm

1 Trace the leaf and flower shapes on the cardboard. Cut these out and draw around them on the appropriate fabrics. For each towel cut 1 flower and 2 leaves. Use light green satin for the dark towels and contrasting thread for the leaves. Use dark green satin for the light towels, again using contrasting thread for the leaves.

2 Draw the veins on the leaves, using chalk or a pencil.

3 Use the design plan as a guide to place leaf no. 1 in the correct position. Pin and baste the shape to the towel. With a small straight stitch, machine stitch around the leaf, keeping close to the raw edge. Begin stitching from the base of the leaf, which will be covered by the flower. Reset the sewing machine to satin stitch or closed zig-zag stitch (width 3 or 4, minimum length) and carefully stitch along the edge of the leaf, covering the raw edge completely and securely.

▢ LEAF SHAPE 1
LAY IN POSITION, PIN, BASTE AND STITCH
(WORK FIRST)

▢ LEAF SHAPE 2
(WORK SECOND)

▢ FLOWER SHAPE
(WORK LAST)

Terri Lawlor

4 Work the central rib and two veins of the leaf in satin stitch, varying the stitch width if desired.

5 Repeat these steps of pinning, basting, straight stitching and satin stitching for the second leaf.

6 Stitch the flower in position in the same way, using a thread contrasting with that used for the leaves.

7 Finally, using tailor's chalk draw the 2 stems on the towel, using the design plan as a guide. (You can use the side of a plate as a guide in drawing the curves.) Work the 2 stems in satin stitch as for the central vein of the leaves, using contrasting thread.

8 Press the towels gently on the wrong side to encourage the stitching to stand out.

Hand-sewn appliqué

If your sewing machine does not do zig-zag stitch you can decorate your towels in the same way, using hand stitching.

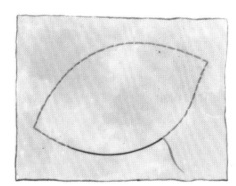

1 Before cutting out shapes, machine stitch along the drawn outline of the shape. This helps to give a smoothly turned-under edge.

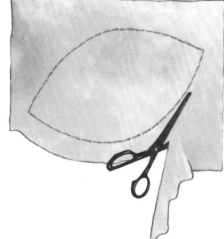

2 Cut out shapes, adding $\frac{1}{4}$in (5mm) outside stitching for seam allowances.

3 Clip seam allowances as shown. Turn under the seam allowance concealing the stitching, baste and press.

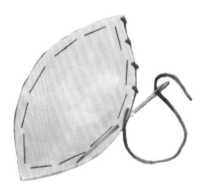

4 Baste the shapes in position on the towel. Attach each shape to the towel using a fine slip stitch.

5 Using a contrasting embroidery thread, such as cotton embroidery floss, stitch around each shape, using a close blanket stitch.

6 Work the stems and the veins of the leaves, using either satin stitch or couching (shown below).

7 To work couching stitch, lay several threads along line. Hold threads taut with left hand, secure with tiny stitches (with one thread in needle), at $\frac{3}{8}$in (1cm) intervals.

Homemaker

Rainbow bathmat

Brighten up bath time with a rainbow mat. Just make up pompoms in a brightly colored synthetic yarn and sew them in rows to a fabric base.

Finished size
28 x 19in (71 x 49cm)
Note 8oz (200g) of yarn will make about 16 pompoms, so for a rug of a different size, adjust quantities accordingly.

Materials
  8oz (200g) of rug yarn in each of the eight colors
  $\frac{7}{8}$yd (.8m) of 36in (90cm)-wide fabric or fine canvas for the backing
  $\frac{7}{8}$yd (.8m) of 36in (90cm)-wide heavyweight iron-on interfacing
  Large bodkin
  Piece of cardboard 7 x 4in (18 x 10cm)
  Thread to match backing fabric

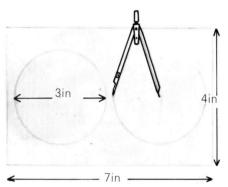

1 On cardboard, mark two 3in (7.5cm)-diameter circles. Cut out each circle carefully.

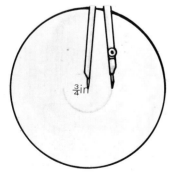

2 In the center of each circle mark a smaller circle with a $\frac{3}{4}$in (2cm) diameter. Cut out each center circle carefully and discard, leaving two rings.
3 From one ball of yarn cut four 6$\frac{1}{2}$yd (6m) lengths.

4 Thread one length of yarn onto the bodkin.

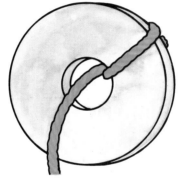

5 Place both cardboard ring templates together. Thread the opposite end of yarn through the center hole of the template. Hold the yarn end firmly in place and take the yarn over the outer part of the template and up through the center hole again.

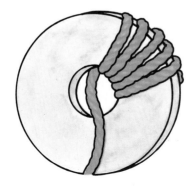

6 Continue as in step 5 winding the yarn around and around the cardboard in the same way, covering it evenly until the yarn is used and the cardboard covered.

Terri Lawlor

Spike Powell

7 Cut a 6in (15cm) length of matching yarn for binding.

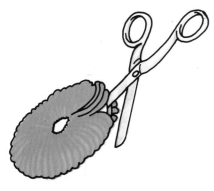

Terry Lawlor

8 Cut through the outer edge of the yarn, between the two circles of cardboard. Slip the 6in (15cm) length of yarn between the two circles and wind it tightly around all the yarn where it passes through the center of the template, and secure.

9 Make 16 pompoms in each of the colors, except for the two colors at each end of the range. Make 14 pompoms in these two colors.

10 From backing fabric cut out one piece for backing 30 x 21 in (75.5 x 53cm).

11 From interfacing cut out one piece 30 x 21 in (75.5 x 53cm).

12 Place the interfacing with shiny side to wrong side of backing fabric, matching all outer edges. Iron in place.

13 Using a pencil and a ruler mark 3in (7.5cm) squares across the interfaced side of the fabric. Start marking the squares from the center outward, leaving a 1½in (4cm) margin all around.

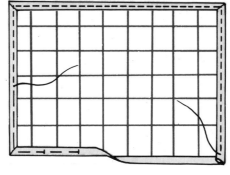

14 On backing fabric, turn under a double $\frac{3}{8}$in (1cm) - wide hem all around, mitering the corners. Pin, baste and stitch in place all around.

15 Sew the pompoms onto the interfaced side of the backing fabric. Position a pompom at each of the pencil intersections and in the center of each square, following the chart for colors. Sew each of the pompoms securely in place.

Key to chart
● red   ○ green
□ orange   ⊠ turquoise
▲ yellow   △ blue
✕ lime   ⊡ royal

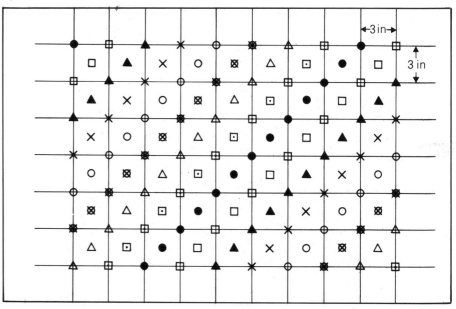